every

day | simple steps to
cultivating

hospitality | a welcoming

heart

thea jarvis

ave maria press  notre dame, indiana

© 2007 by Thea Kielt Jarvis

Founded in 1865, Ave Maria Press is a ministry of the Indiana Province of Holy Cross.

www.avemariapress.com

ISBN-10 1-59471-070-8 ISBN-13 978-1-59471-070-4

Cover photograph © Corbis Images

Cover and text design by Katherine Robinson Coleman

Printed and bound in the United States of America.

Library of Congress Cataloging-in-Publication Data

    Jarvis, Thea.

      Everyday hospitality : simple steps for cultivating a welcoming heart / Thea Jarvis.

      p. cm.

    Includes bibliographical references.

    ISBN-13: 978-1-59471-070-4 (pbk.)

    ISBN-10: 1-59471-070-8 (pbk.)

    1. Hospitality—Religious aspects—Christianity. I. Title.

    BV4647.H67J38 2007

    241'.671—dc22

                                      2006100556

FOR MY PARENTS,

WHO HAVE

ALWAYS MADE

ME WELCOME.

contents

introduction

an

old-fashioned

virtue with

modern

meaning

I must look for my identity,
somehow, not only in God,
but in other men.
I will never be able to find
myself if I isolate myself
from the rest of mankind
as if I were a different
kind of being.

THOMAS MERTON

ospitality may be a familiar, old-fashioned virtue, but it hasn't yet gone out of style. In our homes and communities, schools and churches, families and neighborhoods, hospitality remains the glorious centerpiece of the human dinner table. It's the flag we rally around to remind ourselves that we're all in this together. It's the sturdy thread that binds us gently to each other.

The value and usefulness of hospitality is more apparent than ever. In our fast-paced, ever-mobile society, intimacy is often suppressed by isolation and loneliness.

Widening social and economic gaps foster hunger, homelessness, violence, and fear. Airplanes, cell phones, and e-mail may keep us in touch twenty-four/seven, but we still seek that elusive sense of belonging that makes us feel curiously, joyously, at home.

Admittedly, hospitality won't cure all of our ills. It won't erase underlying problems that promote a climate of division or create a magical panacea for human suffering. But hospitality can help. It can assist and guide us in the way we deal with and ultimately solve our problems. It can allow us to function with grace and dignity.

In our global community, hospitality has become a vital, booming industry. The business side of it makes the world run more smoothly and efficiently, promoting greater productivity and offering choices we might not otherwise have. But lavish hotels, professional catering services, and exclusive vacation packages don't lessen our yearning for the homegrown version. They're welcome, but often short-term fixes that can distract us from our spiritual center and leave us feeling empty. In fact, the proliferation of such commercial outlets for hospitality only makes this basic element of spirituality even more meaningful and attractive.

Hospitality is the social staff of life, a starting point for discourse and interaction. Even when we're not conscious of its presence, hospitality stands by like a gracious host, discreetly ensuring friendly exchanges and peaceful out-comes. It's background music to the human dance, an old song that still rings true.

SEEKING HOSPITALITY

Ideally, hospitality is the outward expression of an inner attitude, a virtue that erupts from the heart, spilling out toward others. A conscious pursuit of hospitality can lead to sanctity because it invariably involves selflessness and sacrifice. Not surprisingly, it's a subject of interest to many who are serious about spiritual growth.

My friends Faye and Jerry exemplify this spiritual side of hospitality. We met when our families were young and we spent long, happy weekends together watching our kids run up and down the soccer fields. I learned that you can accurately test a person's mettle by sharing hard alu-minum bleacher seats with them for hours at a time. Faye and Jerry turned out to be a caring, generous couple. As their youngsters grew up and left the nest, my friends con-tinued to participate in the lives of their children and grandchildren. But they also found the freedom to extend hospitality beyond the boundaries of their own household. Faye now teaches English as a second language at a local college, where she sees commonalities rather than differences among people from other countries. Jerry has reached out as well, reading the Bible with a young Korean as a way for the newcomer to learn English and for both men to reflect on scripture together. "Hospitality reminds me of the importance of personal relationships over tasks," Jerry has found. "Unfortunately, our dominant culture doesn't normally value or encourage this."

When their church decided to offer an adult course in hospitality, Faye and Jerry were tapped as facilitators. Their class explored ancient hospitality codes and traditions and how to apply them to their own circumstances. The group shared personal experiences and heard from experts on foster care, homelessness, and the challenge of single parenthood. "We learned how creative people can be in extending hospitality and how gestures of care and concern have come so naturally to them," said Faye. "It was humbling and encouraging to hear."

Faye and Jerry both agreed that the class not only became more aware of hospitality as a spiritual discipline, but also recognized the genuine difficulty of putting good intentions into practice. Fear of strangers, a limited supply of time and energy, a heavy emphasis on privacy, personal responsibilities, and everyday commitments forced them all to question exactly how hospitality might play out in the midst of their hectic lives.

"It goes far beyond just inviting someone to your home," Faye has discovered. "Practicing hospitality requires thinking of others first and trusting that good will come from what you do."

CLOSE TO HOME

Like Faye and Jerry's Sunday school class, I believe hospitality is worth a closer look. It has nuances I need to ponder and depths I need to plumb. I already know hospitality is a colorful part of the spiritual spectrum, but integrating it into my busy days bears thought and consideration.

Fortunately, over the past few years, hospitality has come knocking on my door like a persistent salesman who won't take no for an answer. I've been forced to throw open the portals because the steady rapping just couldn't be ignored. Once inside my house, bringing family, friends, and all manner of eye-popping scenarios, hospitality made it abundantly clear that it was here to stay.

Sometimes we choose hospitality as a path to spiritual enlightenment. More often than not, hospitality chooses us. For someone like me—relatively inexperienced and often unprepared—basic truths surface quietly, like fireflies on a summer night. Simple maxims remind me of the way hospitality works at the kitchen sink level:

✦ My table can always expand to make room for one more person.

✦ My heart can always expand to make room for one more person.

✦ The kitchen is the most hospitable room in my house.

✦ The person most in need of hospitality may be living under my own roof.

✦ To be effective, hospitality must be balanced with solitude.

✦ Kindness, compassion, and generosity are the marks of hospitality.

✦ To be hospitable is to be an instrument of peace.

The reflections in this book are explorations of the hospitality I've sought to inject into my own life and the hospitality I've been privileged to receive along the way. It's my hope that, in some way, these thoughts will bring a measure of hospitality to your own heart. If so, please accept them as a gift from me to you.

one

what

is

hospitality?

Once a week, without fail, I receive an e-mail from my maternal grandmother. It's usually a synopsis of the latest family news and gossip, along with a reminder to check Grandma's website for an expanded version of her weekly updates. Although technical touches are left to my able cousin Bob, who acts as webmaster, Grandma oversees an amicable exchange of information that makes the site a treat for family members like me to explore.

Grandma is the patron saint of my very large Irish-Catholic family, a spiritual presence whose ardent faith and generous heart have kept us close and strong throughout her lifetime and beyond. Though she died almost forty years ago at the age of seventy-nine, my grandmother continues to be the surest link to my heritage

17

and a cornerstone of the hospitality that's been its hallmark for as long as I can remember.

A quirky photograph of Grandma welcomes clan members who eagerly surf her website and wander its archives. It's an old black and white Polaroid taken by my father in our family kitchen. Seated in a chair near the stove, her shoulders sagging slightly under a soft print dress, Grandma bears an antique pith helmet on her head and a cavalry sword in her right hand. How my parents talked her into sporting such gear is more than I care to know, but the effect is memorable. As Grandma peers out from under the brim of her hard hat with gentle but determined eyes, a knowing smile plays about her face. It's as if she senses the future amusement her picture will inspire. *I'm still here*, she reminds us. *Don't forget me.*

Grandma's progeny haven't forgotten her. Indeed, with the help of modern technology, we've expanded her legacy exponentially. My grandmother's twelve children blessed her with forty-four grandchildren, many of whom are themselves grandparents today. Sixty of these descendants populate her website, which has, over time, evolved into a hotbed of hospitality. Relatives separated by time and geography catch up, reconnect, and meet all kinds of people they never knew were part of their family tree. Digital pictures reveal the friendly faces behind the message boards. In a mysterious mesh of internet visitation, family reunions are planned, new arrivals welcomed, graduations applauded, and weddings commemorated. On Grandma's webpage, milestones that are a significant part of every family's history are now opportunities for communal celebration.

My family boasts some illustrious stars. There's the actor who's been a regular on my favorite television crime show. The design maven whose books and furnishings are found in countless homes and retail outlets across the country. There are artists and builders, financial analysts and legal eagles, doctors and dentists, teachers and insurance adjusters. Yet, at Grandma's website, no one is more important than anyone else. Each person is equally and graciously received. It's as if we're all seated around an oversized harvest table exchanging stories and feeding from my grandmother's well-stocked larder. We're kinfolk relaxing at a web-based barbeque with slaw on the side. Our family website reflects the earthy hospitality Grandma was always eager to dispense. If you were hungry, Grandma fed you. Tired? Go upstairs and take a nap. If you were in need of a wash there were clean towels hanging on the rack and sweet-smelling soap in a porcelain dish. There was always room for another mouth at dinner, always another potato that could be used to pad a meal. At Grandma's, hospitality was homegrown and heartfelt. Under her roof, wants were quietly anticipated and quickly met.

I was fortunate enough to experience firsthand the gift of my grandmother's hospitality. As an infant, my mother and I sheltered at Grandma's house while my father flew reconnaissance blimps out of California during World War II. Later, when I returned for childhood visits, I was pampered like a princess and coddled like a queen. Deaf to my own ear-shattering plunking, I played Grandma's piano early and late. I ate cherry buns for breakfast and savored tea biscuits before bed. Grandma's penny jar existed solely for my benefit and her old clothes were saved especially for my carefree dress-up days. At Grandma's, I danced and sang to music that told me I was all I needed to be. I felt safe and secure, welcomed and loved, cherished and accepted.

To this day, the hospitality I experienced in my grandmother's home is the benchmark by which I judge all other expressions of this virtue. It is, perhaps, the source of my own interest in the subject and the example I try hardest to emulate. True hospitality, like my grandmother's, is unpretentious and warm, generous and encouraging—a natural manifestation of inner unselfishness. One of the simplest, most basic of disciplines, hospitality asks only that I be open to and accepting of others, willing to move over and make space for someone else at the table of life.

MUTUALITY OF HOSPITALITY

Hospitality is a virtue, an element of spirituality that involves a warm and often tender exchange between people. In a world that can be cold and unfeeling, hospitality is a blessing and a comfort. Most certainly, it is a gift.

Have you ever watched a group of two-year-olds playing together? In their greedy innocence, they are loath to share, protective of their own toys, eager to take possession of everyone else's treasure. "Mine!" they bellow vehemently, often adding a well-placed smack to a playmate's head for emphasis. Toddlers haven't yet mastered the nuts and bolts of hospitable interaction or realized its merits. They haven't yet learned that the official definition of hospitality involves the friendly, generous entertainment of guests. Little ones must be taught, their self-centeredness honed and molded by wise and watchful elders.

But once directed to do the right thing, even young children understand the payoff hospitality offers: *If I give you my truck, you'll give me your train. If I let you ride in my wagon, I can ride on your trike. If I share with you, you share with me.* Even if a child's hospitality has more to do with the loss of a lollipop or the threat of time out than the ethics of exchange, the lesson is nevertheless learned: kindness begets kindness, goodness fosters goodness, generosity can't help but sow its fruitful seed in others.

Hospitality is contagious. Like a benevolent virus with pandemic potential, it bewitches us with its charm, infects us with its potency, enthralls us with its expansiveness. It's a mark of civilized society, a sign of cultural advancement, a badge of spiritual enlightenment. Without hospitality, we remain in a dark cave of seclusion and separation, where the lights are out and the heat is never turned on. In hospitality's embrace, we're warmed by the glow of a communal fire, illuminated by sparks of empathy and compassion.

When writer and theologian Henri Nouwen traded his scholarly life at Harvard for a pastor-ship at a Toronto community for the disabled in 1986, his role as caregiver was matched in kind by the hospitality he received from those in his care. In particular, he found that his relationship with Adam, a mentally and physically handicapped young man whose every need he tended to on a daily basis, became an avenue to inner peace.

"I started to realize that there was a mutuality of love not based on shared knowledge or shared feelings, but on shared humanity," writes Nouwen in his reflection, *The Path to Peace*. Bathing, dressing, and feeding Adam at Daybreak was labor-intensive and emotionally demanding. Communication was unattainable in the conventional sense since Adam, who was unable to walk and feed himself, could not speak. It took the highest level of patience and acceptance for Nouwen to achieve a connection with this person who was entirely dependent upon him for his most essential needs.

Before coming to Daybreak, part of a network of L'Arche communities founded by Jean Vanier in 1964, Nouwen had become a burnt-out case. Torn by multi-layered responsibilities to his teaching, writing and mission work, he had sunk into depression and spiritual dryness. His arrival at L'Arche serendipitously placed him within a circle of hospitality that enabled him to heal even as he shared in the healing of others. Nouwen's gentle care of Adam, combined with Adam's peaceful acceptance of Nouwen's ministrations, forged a union in which the roles of caregiver and receiver evolved into a mutual ministry of presence. In the peaceful ebb and flow of their interaction, Nouwen's spirit reawakened like a dry fern refreshed with cool water. His tenure at Daybreak, a decade before his death in 1996, was one of the most productive and serene times of his life.

I have never been asked to care for someone with Adam's overwhelming needs, but I have, like Henri Nouwen, experienced the gifts that inevitably follow if I integrate the virtue of hospitality into my personal journey. When hospitality becomes a priority, when I am as faithful to its practice as I am to my morning walk or weekly yoga class, I reap surprising benefits of strength and balance. Often, I experience joy.

Unpredictability of Hospitality

When my husband and I retired to a small island off the Georgia coast, I had some sense that my little corner of paradise might be an attractive destination for friends and family. "We need room for our children and grandchildren," we told the talented architect who shoehorned our cottage into its small, oak-treed lot. He gave us what we needed, even as he joked about ordering an oversized water heater that wouldn't run cold. "You might want to think about making things too comfortable for your guests," he advised. "They may not want to go home."

Such an outcome never developed, but we did notice that the peace and tranquility we had found in our island sanctuary were exactly what the world beyond the causeway was sadly missing. My parents moved down the street; our daughters now live within shouting distance; our sons, just a half-day's drive away, visit often with their wives and children. My gratitude for the gift of my family's presence is exceeded only by my humility in the face of their love and affection.

Happily, our sisters and brothers visit, too. Sometimes, their children and grandchildren plan an island stop, which means several generations of our family might gather in the space of a week, a month, or a year. Recently, my northern cousins have begun to schedule island layovers on their way to or from Florida. Old friends from Atlanta and beyond continue to bless us with their company, as do former business associates and college roommates.

It has been more than I'd hoped for. And more than I expected. We now refer to our house as "The Jarvis Inn." Our walls and windows have been christened with tiny fingerprints; the oak treads on our stairs have lost some of their gloss. There's a dent in the garage door and a slight warp in the kitchen floor from the sink's untimely over-flow. Our home is played in, eaten in, and slept in. Fortunately, I've learned to live in it, too.

My transformation from an imagined *grand dame* of hospitality into a relaxed and welcoming keeper of the key has been gradual and not without struggle. My idea of a tidy house has given way to the temporary chaos that ensues when beloved grandchildren or close friends come to call. Meals may now be last minute, informal, and off the cuff. Plans are permitted to change, bedtimes adapted to seasonal activity and weather reports. Thankfully, my insides have softened as my experience of hospitality has deepened. I don't develop a knot in my stomach if I've for-gotten to plug in the coffeepot or put out extra pillows in the guest room. I'm not quite so frazzled when vacationing feet trail beach sand through my living room or wet towels pile up in the laundry like alien invaders just off the moth-er ship.

The more I'm willing to forego lofty notions of what hospitality *ought* to be and open myself to what hospitality *might* and *could* be, I'm a gentler, kinder, happier host. If I surrender to the magic of the moment and the promptings of the present, hospitality washes over me like water on a rock—rounding me out and putting curves on my angles. It shapes me into someone I wasn't capable of becoming before its gifts and challenges came barreling through my door.

"We can never be completely whole in and of ourselves," psychiatrist M. Scott Peck writes in his book, *The Different Drum*. "We are inevitably social creatures who desperately need each other, not merely for sustenance, not merely for company, but for any meaning to our lives whatsoever."

I know this to be true today. My need for others and their need for me doesn't mean I'm a weak-kneed pariah. I'm connected to you and you to me because that's the way God made us. Hospitality is a natural outgrowth of my membership in the human family. It's a hands-on, open-armed virtue rooted in an instinct to grow beyond my inner landscape, like a flower turning its face to the sun. It demands my availability and attention, my flexibility and spontaneity. Unpredictable, often capricious, hospitality may mean wiping my grandson's runny nose one day and babysitting for my daughter's golden retriever the next. It might have me on my knees scrubbing bathrooms before company comes or up to my elbows cooking Super Bowl chili before the big game. Hospitality means sharing a loss or meeting friends for lunch, greeting a new neighbor or listening patiently to a troubled child. It can be as mundane as putting cereal in the kids' breakfast bowls or as altruistic as serving soup to the homeless. Sometimes sublime, sometimes ridiculous, the blessings of hospitality are as authentic as they are varied. They are most often learned without schooling or study, but never without practice.

12-2-22

SCENES AND SAYINGS

Scriptural examples of hospitality have long offered clear, colorful models of generosity and compassion. For me, they remain the most attractive of biblical passages. Abraham, our nomadic patriarch in faith, receives the promise of a son after he eagerly extends hospitality to visiting strangers, one of whom he eventually recognizes as his Lord. The Old Testament scene depicts an aging Abraham and his wife, Sarah, hurriedly preparing a meal for three men passing by their tent (Gn 18:1–9). Encouraging his guests to bathe their feet and rest under a nearby tree while bread is baked, a steer is roasted, and milk is served, Abraham observes the ancient, unwritten laws of hospitality. Later, he's rewarded with news that, despite his advanced age and Sarah's apparent infertility, they are soon to become parents. "I will surely return to you in due season, and your wife Sarah shall have a son," the Lord informs him. What a happy surprise for this hard-working host! What a strong reminder that hospitality often reaps surprising rewards.

In ancient Israel, rules and ritual held sway, but compassion and hospitality did as well. "When you reap the harvest of your land," the Israelites were cautioned, "you shall not reap to the very edges of your field, or gather the gleanings of your harvest. You shall not strip your vineyard bare, or gather the fallen grapes of your vineyard; you shall leave them for the poor and the alien," beneficiaries of the community's hospitable heart (Lv 19:9–10).

One of my favorite Old Testament passages acknowledges the worthy woman who tends her household with care and devotion, observing a daily routine of love and labor that is a model of hospitality. She is one whose value is "far more precious than jewels," a wife and mother who not only puts food on her family's table and blankets on their beds, but "opens her hand to the poor, and reaches out her hands to the needy" (Prv 31:10–31). This ancient matriarch surely embodies the prophet's admonition to "share your bread with the hungry, and bring the homeless poor into your house; when you see the naked . . . cover them . . . and [do] not . . . hide yourself from your own kin" (Is 58:7–10).

Themes of hospitality have equal or greater significance in the New Testament. When Jesus takes pity on the hungry crowd that has followed him for days and decides it's time for a substantial meal of bread and fish (Mt 15:32–38), I understand that physical needs are as important as spiritual ones and should be honored and satisfied. When Zacchaeus, the little-loved tax collector, climbs down from a sycamore tree to host the Son of Man at his modest table (Lk 19:1–10), I learn that an unexpected call to hospitality is often God's way of getting my attention and teaching me humility. When a youthful Mary visits Elizabeth because her older cousin can't manage household duties during her difficult pregnancy (Lk 1:39–45), I am awed by Mary's goodness. By all accounts, Mary is in the early stages of her own pregnancy, perhaps deep in the throes of morning sickness, when she takes on Elizabeth's unwashed dishes. Her remarkable kindness is a reminder that God always gives me enough strength to do the things I'm asked.

The wedding feast at Cana, the celebrated event that marked Christ's first miracle (Jn 2:1–11), has always struck me as one of Jesus' most hospitable moments. The circumstances can't have differed markedly from contemporary nuptials, at least in the flavor of the festivities and the planning that precedes them. The scene is uncannily familiar. The reception's a hit, the guests are enjoying themselves. The bride and groom inhabit that blissful bubble that for now is theirs alone. But the father of the bride? For him the party's over, the well has run dry. At any moment, formerly smiling guests will turn to whining and complaining. There are two, maybe three cups of wine left in the casks. What to do?

The description of Mary taking her son aside and boldly requesting his help strikes me as the perfect rendering. As the mother of two sons, I've had more than one occasion to enlist their aid in a moment of crisis. They have never let me down, never disappointed. My maternal pleas have always been answered with generosity and faithfulness on their part. Jesus' reaction to Mary mirrors my own experience. Sensitive to his mother, mindful of his hosts' predicament, Jesus puts himself on the line and prevents an unthinkable social disaster. He accommodates himself to the call of hospitality and opens the door to his own identity. Wine flows, music plays, the dancing continues, and the father of the bride breathes an audible sigh of relief.

SCRIPTURAL VALUES

When Jesus teaches about hospitality, he cautions against snobbery and self-promotion. Don't seek out places of honor, he tells invited guests. If you're the host, don't try to impress wealthy neighbors and fussy relatives with favorite recipes and fancy silverware. Instead, turn to the crippled, the poor, the blind, and the lame outside your door. Invite them to your table, Jesus suggests, for "you will be blessed . . . you will be repaid at the resurrection of the righteous" (Lk 14:7–14).

In the Acts of the Apostles, the hospitality of early Christians is recounted as proof of their discipleship. They were "of one heart and soul," living out their faith in a community where possessions were shared and monies distributed as individual needs surfaced (Acts 4:32–35).

New Testament epistles continue the theme: "If a brother or sister is naked and lacks daily food, and one of you says to them, 'Go in peace; keep warm and eat your fill,' and yet you do not supply their bodily needs, what is the good of that?" (Jas 2:14–16). Peter's first epistle states, "Be hospitable to one another without complaining. Like good stewards of the manifold grace of God, serve one another with whatever gift each of you has received" (1 Pet 4:9–10). In his letter to the Romans, Paul counsels his disciples to "love one another with mutual affection; outdo one another in showing honor. . . . Contribute to the needs of the saints; extend hospitality to strangers" (Rom 12:10, 13).

Biblical paradigms of hospitality are part of contemporary thought and language. A *Good Samaritan* (Lk 10:30–37) is shorthand for a person who goes out of his way to help someone in need. A *Judas*, on the other hand, is someone who betrays the hospitality of another (Mt 26:23–25, 47–49).

A *prodigal son* is a child who rejects the love and care of a nurturing family, only to be welcomed back with unconditional hospitality, forgiveness and acceptance (Lk 15:11–24).

Throughout Scripture, hospitality is encouraged as a duty to others and a spiritual path for ourselves. It's also endorsed as a happy occupation that blesses lives and enriches relationships. Biblical hospitality demands that we go the extra mile, welcoming not only friends and family, but strangers and outcasts as well. It is, according to Christine Pohl, author of *Making Room: Recovering Hospitality as a Christian Tradition*, a way to topple social barriers and extend to others the kind of love God extends to us.

Early Church Fathers swapped the noise and bustle of the city for the solitude of the desert. In the empty, arid regions of Egypt, Arabia, and Palestine, they carved out a life of prayer and meditation, often as hermits whose contact with others was infrequent and unsought. Nonetheless, writes Thomas Merton in *Wisdom of the Desert*, fourth century Fathers carefully followed the norms of biblical hospitality. "Charity and hospitality were matters of top priority and took precedence over fasting and personal ascetic routines," notes Merton, who himself embraced the eremitic life during a portion of his Trappist vocation. In his informal translation of their words and stories, he deftly captures the rock-solid spirituality that guided these saintly heroes of early Christianity.

When a brother monk came to stay with one of the hermits, Merton writes, the visitor felt he had intruded on the solitary routine of his fellow. As he was leaving, he humbly asked forgiveness for imposing on the hermit's time and rations. He was met, however, with the kindest of replies. "My Rule is to receive you with hospitality and to let you go in peace," his host proclaimed as he bid his guest farewell.

Another passage tells of two brethren who stopped in on an elder more accustomed to fasting than to eating regularly. Setting aside his usual habits, the elder joyfully welcomed his visitors and invited them to dine with him. "Fasting has its own reward," said the elder wisely, "but he who eats out of charity fulfills two commandments, for he sets aside his own will and he refreshes his hungry brethren."

The message from such texts is delightfully clear: hospitality is to be chosen even above spiritual practices that appear more noble and worthwhile, more high-minded and ethereal. In most cases, hospitality trumps prayer and solitude, fasting and sacrifice. It's a primary virtue, a matter of significance to those traveling the realist's road to perfection. Like an old silver spoon stored in soft gray flannel, hospitality neither dulls with time nor discolors with wear. It shines the brighter when brought to the table and used with regularity.

INDIVIDUALITY OF HOSPITALITY

Hospitality is not unlike the pink, blue, and yellow Play-Doh our kids and grandkids love to squish between their fingers and ball up in their pudgy little hands. One minute it's a pancake, the next it's a heart-shaped valentine. To the clever, it's a little blue man or a yellow rabbit. To a curious toddler, it's something new to eat. The shape and purpose of Play-Doh, much like the shape and purpose of hospitality, is determined by circumstance and the personality of the shaper.

Because we're all called to hospitality in our own space and time, what we have to offer will be as unique and personal as the print of our finger, the bridge of our nose, the smile on our face. We're blessed with opportunities to integrate hospitality into our lives in ways that no one else has and no one else can.

The corporal and spiritual works of mercy, guides to good works and unselfishness based on the words of Jesus in the Gospel of Matthew, have about them the familiar ring of hospitality. They cover a wide panorama of compassion and concern: feeding the hungry, giving drink to the thirsty, clothing the naked, sheltering the homeless, visiting the sick, ransoming the captive, burying the dead, as well as instructing the ignorant, counseling the doubtful, admonishing sinners, bearing wrongs patiently, forgiving offenses willingly, comforting the afflicted, and praying for the living and the dead. These generous actions, daunting as they might seem when viewed as a whole, are simply ways to put hospitality to work in everyday life. I may not admonish sinners on a weekly basis, but there might be a time when a sorrowful soul crosses my path in need of encouragement and forgiveness. To that person, I can offer a listening heart and the benefit of my own experience, strength, and hope. Likewise, there aren't many folks passing unclothed and unfed down my street, but I can recycle the clothes in my closet, the linens on my shelf, the canned soup in my pantry for those in my community who can surely use them. Living out the works of mercy isn't always straightforward or easily done. It takes practice to identify opportunities and strike an acceptable balance between generosity and foolhardiness.

Many years ago, when my oldest son was in preschool, I noticed that one of his classmates wore only a light jacket on a blustery winter day. When I mentioned how cold the boy must be, his teacher explained that the child's family couldn't afford a warmer coat. Eager to lend a hospitable hand, I returned home and helped myself to the bounty of my son's closet, certain it held a solution to the problem at hand. There, among the jeans, shirts, shoes, and caps, I found a blue storm coat that not only looked like a good fit for the little boy, but also had a dandy zip-on hood for added warmth.

The coat was a couple of years old, but still in good repair. Since my son had worn another jacket to school that morning, I deemed the blue coat an extra. I was convinced that Saint Basil the Great's rule of thumb applied here: "The bread which you do not use is the bread of the hungry; the garment hanging in your wardrobe is that of one who is naked; the shoes you do not wear are those of one who is barefoot; the acts of charity you do not perform are so many injustices that you commit."

Back at school for the usual noontime pickup, I quietly slipped my son's blue coat into the teacher's hands and asked that she turn it over to the needy child. The preschool staff was delighted with my thoughtfulness, happy to dispense such a tangible symbol of hospitality. "He can really use it," they assured me, their gratitude touching my heart and flattering my ego. On the way home, I proudly informed my son that his blue coat was no longer hanging in the closet but was now warming his classmate's cold and narrow frame. His reaction to my largesse was unexpected.

"Why did you give away my coat?" he exploded, his blue eyes filling with angry tears. Too late, I realized that he wasn't interested in the rules of selflessness, the demands of biblical hospitality, the elusive ideals of his misguided mother. He hadn't read Saint Basil and I was no less than a thief who'd sneaked into his private storehouse and fingered a favorite possession.

Today, my son and I can smile about the loss of his blue coat. He has, I believe, forgiven me for the indiscretion I committed in the name of good works and hospitality. I can't however, forget my disregard for his rights and feelings. The child in that long-ago school playground was warmer for the winter jacket, but my son was colder for its loss. I shouldn't have donated what wasn't mine to give, however honorable my motive. Far better to have let the coat's owner decide if he was ready to let it go. Far better to have driven to the mall and picked out a brand new coat for the little boy whose parents didn't have the means to do so themselves.

There's an art to hospitality not found between the covers of etiquette books or home and garden magazines. Motivation counts, but sensitivity counts more. It's a fine balance I'm still trying to achieve, but others point the way.

BLESSINGS OF HOSPITALITY

On a recent Thanksgiving, my friend Carol wasn't feeling terribly thankful. Earlier in the month, her home had been ransacked by burglars who'd not only made off with irreplaceable family heirlooms, but vandalized her house as well. It was taking weeks to repair windows, flooring, even walls marred by the most inhospitable of guests. Carol's husband, a chef, was serving turkey and dressing to hungry restaurant patrons that day, so our family invited Carol to sample our holiday fare. We'd planned a large gathering at my daughter's house, an informal *al fresco* potluck with tables lined end to end in the breezeway and a backyard picnic table for little ones who preferred to eat with their fingers. We noshed our way through several courses before we realized that there was no sign of Carol. Only after we began clearing the dessert dishes did she arrive, her happy grin assuring us that all was well.

"I got lost," Carol admitted, still smiling but clearly breathless from her search. "I went to the wrong house and thought it was yours." She had indeed gone to the wrong house. In fact, she'd gotten through its front door and was seated at a stranger's table before she'd realized where she was. Or perhaps where she wasn't. "I looked around and didn't know anyone," she related between giggles. "They didn't know me either, but I guess I looked hungry. They told me I was very welcome to stay on and have dinner with them." Declining their offer with sheepish thanks, Carol left the neighbor's home with a hopeful spirit and a roomful of new friends.

For me, the most striking part of Carol's adventure wasn't its uncanny similarity to a television sitcom or its obvious potential as a video blooper, but the generous welcome she received. Her Thanksgiving hosts raised no objections and asked no questions, but made room at their table for an unknown, uninvited, unexpected guest. If Carol thought she belonged there, who were they to say she didn't? Their unconditional acceptance was an example made stronger for the good humor that surrounded it. At the end of the day, Carol had plenty to eat and much to be grateful for. We all gained a new perspective on the holiday and the hospitality that always makes it memorable.

When I ponder the meaning of hospitality, it's Carol's Thanksgiving that comes to mind. And my grandmother's kitchen. And the loved ones who cross my threshold each season. Such magical moments are the opportunities hospitality offers, the blessings it bestows, the promises it keeps.

Hospitality is a virtue both ancient and new. Its element of surprise keeps us open to possibilities and in touch with the world around us. At its heart is a longing to extend to others the gracious welcome we ourselves hope to receive.

we're already

practicing

hospitality

> I have always wanted to
> have a neighbor just
> like you!
>
> I've always wanted to live in
> a neighborhood with you.
>
> Fred Rogers

Many a morning over the past few years, as I sat on my front porch sipping a first cup of tea, I often saw my neighbor Judy whiz by in her tan Chrysler. Judy, I knew, was off to check on her elderly mother, who still lived in her own home despite ongoing health problems requiring round the clock oversight. Judy relieved the night caregiver and did some light housekeeping, assisted her mom with a shower, and fixed her breakfast before daytime help arrived. In the evening, Judy and her husband returned to have supper with her mother and wish her a warm good night. When Judy's mother died peacefully at the age of ninety-two, Judy was there, as she had been all along.

Every Friday, my parents fix grilled cheese sandwiches for dinner. Dad does the cooking, though Mom's in charge of the bread, which has to be fresh, thick, and hearty enough to satisfy big appetites. Dad slices the onions and mounds them atop the cheese, along with tomatoes and lots of butter. If you had the great good luck to try one of these sandwiches, you'd count them among the best you've ever eaten. In fact, if you stopped by my parents' house on a typical Friday night, you'd most certainly be invited to savor the family fare. In Mom and Dad's humble culinary opinion, grilled cheese suppers taste better when shared.

Each Tuesday, my husband volunteers at the local St. Vincent de Paul Society thrift store. There, he's a jack of all trades, picking up furniture donations, sorting clothes, even acting as translator for some newly arrived Hispanic families. Some days he'll be on cleanup detail; on other days you'll find him hanging shelves or curtain rods. He offers his time and energy because, for him, it's a hands-on way to connect with his community.

These dear people, so close to my heart, might not see themselves as paragons of hospitality. Perhaps they'd be embarrassed if I told them they were living out a primary element of spirituality and pursuing a sacred goal. But their extraordinary practice of welcoming, seamlessly integrated into the fabric of their days, is nothing less than the quiet pulse of hospitality, beating steadily, fueling their inner lives. Like a secret treasure hidden under the floorboards of their souls, hospitality has been there all along, animating and enriching them, encouraging them to be just a little bit more than they thought they could be.

OPPORTUNITIES FOR HOSPITALITY

Sometimes, hospitality hovers in the wings, waiting for a chance to take center stage. Like a well-trained understudy who longs to be part of a Broadway bonanza, hospitality is ready for action whenever the call comes. Usually, its script plays out with grace and ease.

A few years ago, members of my parish realized that one of our own was spending an inordinate amount of time in the day chapel. People who stopped by the church to pray invariably found a gentle, white-haired lady smiling at them from the back pew. Over time, her story came to light. Though her family had given her a place to stay each evening, they asked her to remain out of the house during the day. They also limited her access to their phone and refrigerator. Isolated and alone, with no means of transportation and not much to do, this humble lady discovered that a morning walk to church gave her safe refuge and the warmth of familiar faces.

Instinctively, people responded with compassionate practicality. Following a cordial dialogue with the woman's relatives, parishioners found and helped furnish a modest, affordable flat that perfectly suited her needs.

Rides to church and the grocery store were also provided. A circle of friendship and support soon surrounded this deserving lady whose awkward living arrangement had put her life on hold. She was no longer a semi-homeless victim of adverse circumstance, but an independent person whose significance had been acknowledged and appreciated by others. Today, she still finds the little chapel a place of welcome. But because of the hospitality that revived and restored her, she's now at home wherever she goes.

The clear and apparent need of another is the most common motivation for practicing hospitality. It beckons like a siren song, disarming and attracting us, urging us on. Before we know it, our focus has shifted and we're going out of our way to accommodate someone other than ourselves.

How often and how easily do we set aside our own interests and put someone else first? The supermarket shopper with a quart of milk and loaf of bread in his hands is invited to cut ahead of another with a basketful of groceries. A driver merging into morning traffic is signaled forward by a considerate commuter who slows down to let him in. Neighbors who forgot to cancel their newspaper before taking the kids to Disneyland are saved from a cluttered front yard and possible burglary by the kindly couple next door. Such gestures, almost unconscious and usually unplanned, are clear signs that we've got a jump-start on hospitality, that the welcome mat is out and company's expected. This most accessible of virtues bears the friendly face of familiarity because it's already a big part of our lives.

MEMORIES OF HOSPITALITY

The first time I visited my future husband's home, we were both college students, still getting to know each other and just beginning to know each other's families. His parents were quiet New Englanders, unaccustomed to eligible young ladies showing up at their doorstep for long weekends. Unlike my large, gregarious family, theirs was small and less chatty. They had a puffy yellow-haired cat named Goldie, whose lovely coat of fur, alas, caused my allergies to ignite, and a collection of antique furniture that, even in my youth, I could appreciate. There was a crocheted afghan on the loveseat and African violets in the bay window, a spooky cellar where potatoes were stored and a second story where my husband's favorite aunt and uncle lived.

We all did our best to smile and be friendly. Even the cat made himself at home in my bed. But breaking the ice is always chilly business. Like walking around a newly poured path, we're careful how and where we step. Everything and everyone in my sweetheart's home was strange and new to me, just as I was strange and new to them. Thankfully, things became more comfortable when I spied a dish of chocolate-covered cream drops on the living room coffee table.

"You like chocolate, I see," my future mother-in-law observed as I popped a second cream drop in my mouth. "I *love* chocolate!" I exclaimed, voicing the understatement of the century while checking out the remaining supply. Her smile was indulgent and genuine. Sitting in the living room, a state of sugary bliss slowly replacing my unbridled anxiety, I relaxed for the first time that weekend.

The cream drops were a point of connection for my husband's family and me. On subsequent visits, which occurred more and more frequently as our courtship continued and our engagement became official, his parents always left cream drops out on the coffee table. They were, I knew, especially for me. The bottomless container of chocolate delight was their way of saying, *Welcome! We accept and approve of you. We're glad you're going to be part of our family*. Though unspoken, their message expressed a universal language of hospitality I could easily understand.

When my husband-to-be arrived at my house for the first time, things were different. Dogs and children gadded about. Three floors and a basement presented a mysterious maze of rooms and stairways to the uninitiated guest.

Relatives came and went like traffic at a stoplight, and meals resembled a gathering of the Waltons. When dinnertime rolled around, my mother cooked her standard fare: four vegetables and a roast that could have fed the neighborhood. My husband, always appreciative of a good meal, made short work of his plate. He even ate the zucchini.

"How did you like the squash?" asked my mother, eager to please this handsome addition to our family table. "It was good, very good," he replied. Always taught to eat everything put before him, he had conscientiously polished off the zucchini even though it was far from his favorite veggie. Throughout our dating years and even after our marriage, my mother continued to present an oversized platter of zucchini whenever my husband and I came to dinner. Convinced that her son-in-law relished every mouthful, she made extra helpings just for him. Only after some twenty years of ritual zucchini eating did my spouse work up the courage to speak the truth: *Enough with the squash! I'm overcome with your welcoming ways. I understand that you love me, but let's try some green beans tonight.*

Thankfully, he and my mom both had a good laugh and zucchini became an unlikely cornerstone of their relationship. Today, their solid friendship is based on honesty and mutual respect, proving to me that even when it takes a wrong turn, hospitality rarely falls on its face if it's offered for the right reasons.

ON THE ROAD

In so-called primitive cultures, the practice of hospitality was an honored discipline. Indigenous peoples had a heightened sense of duty to the stranger in their midst. Often, separate rooms or structures were set aside for travelers needing a place to rest before continuing on their journey. People were welcomed and graciously received, food was offered without thought of recompense. To turn away a visitor was to break an unwritten code of community conduct. Today, hospitality may be less structured, but it's no less valued as a social norm. Visitors continue to experience hospitality in contemporary settings that have become the modern era's version of an ancient tradition.

Nowhere have I found this to be truer than when I've traveled. Nowhere have I felt more dependent on the good will and hospitality of others than when I myself have been the stranger, unfamiliar with my surroundings and unsure of my bearings. Almost always, I've discovered that hospitality is alive and well, living in the hearts and hands of people I'm lucky enough to meet on my journey.

A recent trip to the southwestern United States took my husband and me far from home over the Easter holidays. I was delighted to explore the awe-inspiring sights of the Colorado plateau, but homesick for our usual family brunch and egg hunt, the comfort of friendly faces and loving arms. On Easter Sunday, we found ourselves at San Felipe de Neri, the historic church on Albuquerque's picturesque town square. The little structure was packed to overflowing with extended families and groups of tourists, all eager to celebrate the feast. Blessed with a clear, sunny spring day, chattering children and busy grownups arrived early to get a seat. Microphones magnified the excited whisperings of the church's youth choir. Ushers busied themselves with latecomers hurrying through the doors.

When a woman behind me returned her kneeler to an upright position, it collided noisily with my foot. Gingerly, I sat back and felt a tentative hand on my shoulder. "I'm so sorry," the embarrassed lady said with a rueful grin. "Our old church has a lot of creaky equipment." She asked if we were visiting and shared her own story of moving from the northeast five years earlier. Her daughter lived in Durango, she said, and she'd been coming to Albuquerque for many years, drawn to its friendly, casual atmosphere and scenic treasures. "I miss New York terribly," she admitted, "but I feel so much at home here."

Our lively conversation continued until the congregation was called to order by the choir director, who invited regular parishioners to stand up and be counted. "Now everyone else is a visitor," she said of those who remained seated, "so let's all introduce ourselves and find out where we're from." The previous hum of fidgeting bodies and twiddling thumbs was overlaid with the sounds of some three hundred people exchanging information, exclaiming over coincidences that linked them like loops in a daisy chain. In that crowded space filled with hundreds of folks I barely knew, I'd never felt more comfortable.

It has been said that there are no strangers, only friends we've yet to meet. When hospitality is practiced with the unselfconscious warmth and enthusiasm I experienced in San Felipe, I know this to be true. Our connectedness, our spiritual kinship is at the core of our human impulse to reach out and extend the hand of hospitality to others. "True joy is hidden where we are the same as other people: fragile and mortal," Henri Nouwen reminds us in *Bread for the Journey*. "It is the joy of belonging to the human race. It is the joy of being with others as a friend, a companion, a fellow traveler."

GOING THE DISTANCE

Hospitality given and received is an outgrowth of everyday living, a natural expression of our social and spiritual selves. Like breathing, it's most often done without thought or expectation, most often achieved without excitement or fanfare. Sometimes, however, we're dizzied by the heights and depths we reach when hospitality calls. We're startled by the surprising places to which hospitality leads us. And when we finally arrive at these unimagined destinations, these uncanny circumstances that have inserted themselves into our lives, we're usually relieved to discover that we're exactly where we're supposed to be.

My old friends Rose and Lou were busy raising a family in the mid-1970s when countless South Vietnamese refugees sought U.S. shelter in the aftermath of war. These newly arrived immigrants, many of whom had served in the military or had worked for the American government, fled political reprisal with no more than the few belongings they'd hastily packed before their escape. Those who landed on American soil were adopted by churches and civic groups that helped regroup and resettle them. For Rose and Lou, Atlantans who had long been sympathetic to the plight of the Vietnamese people, their presence in this country was a chance to make a difference.

My friends participated in a local outreach to eight young Vietnamese adults. With others in their church community, they helped these newcomers find housing and jobs, taught them language skills, and provided transportation when needed. As time went on, one young man absorbed more and more of their attention.

"We began to focus on Cong and soon brought him to the house at least one evening each week," Lou recalled. Cong, he explained, always seemed to be stressed by his circumstances, missing his brothers and sisters still living in

Vietnam and overwhelmed by the challenges of his new life in America. Cong's physical health was an issue as well. One day, when Lou stopped by Cong's apartment to pick him up for their usual family night, Cong was too weak to move. "Clearly," said Lou, "something needed to be done quickly or we were destined for a serious problem."

After a family caucus, Rose and Lou invited Cong to live in their home. "They all thought it was a good idea," Lou remembered. Cong would bunk with their young son, then six, who was thrilled to have a big brother. Their nine-year-old twin girls and oldest daughter, aged twelve, already felt at ease with Cong and were glad for his presence. Rose, a nurse who believed a gastric ulcer caused Cong's digestive difficulties, was happy to oversee his diet and medication. Under a doctor's care and the family's watchful eye, Cong was able to strengthen and heal.

"We found a store that carried Chinese food and bought Ramen noodles by the case," said Lou. "Then we located some lychee nuts and all was well." Cong became increasingly relaxed with his new friends, and as his health improved, he returned to work at a local garden center. "He very easily began to function as a member of our family," Lou recalled. "Having the children around seemed to make him feel part of something that he had left behind as he scrambled aboard a helicopter just a few months before."

Cong saved enough money to purchase a car, which allowed him a freedom he never abused. He'd always call Rose and Lou if he was going to be late for dinner or if an evening with friends was planned. When Rose and Lou held a birthday party for Cong a year after his arrival, they included a large group of his Vietnamese countrymen who had managed to locate and support each other in their new land. "Two brothers sponsored by a local Lutheran church moved massive sound equipment into our den, along with strobe lights, crepe paper and decorations," said Lou. "It was one of the largest gatherings of Vietnamese people we'd yet experienced."

Cong lived with his American family for more than two years. The hospitality they provided gave him the security and stability he needed to move out on his own and achieve greater autonomy. Over time, these bonds of friendship deepened. When Cong became engaged, he asked Lou to act on behalf of Cong's deceased father. It was a duty Lou gamely undertook and carried out with pride. "In an entourage of cars decorated with flowers and ribbons, we drove to the future bride's house," he said. "There we ceremoniously met with her family and accepted the dowry, sharing food and drink for hours. We went through a similar ritual for their Buddhist wedding months later."

Cong eventually bought a shoe repair shop in a midtown Atlanta mall and Lou helped out as needed, filling in when his friend was ill or out of town. After Cong's wife delivered their first child, she went straight from the hospital to Rose and Lou's home, where she was treated to a week of care and tutoring in baby basics. Rose and Lou accompanied Cong to the hospital when he required heart valve surgery, and when Lou himself was unexpectedly hospitalized, Cong was one of the first to stop by and check on his friend.

Today, Cong and his wife, the proud parents of two beautiful daughters, have steady jobs and a home not far from Rose and Lou's own suburban neighborhood. "Cong remains part of our family," said Lou. "Our children look upon him as their brother, and he and his family are always included in our celebrations." Cong's future looks bright because one selfless couple followed the road map of hospitality to an unexpected, unexplored destination. "It's been an unbelievable journey we couldn't have anticipated back in 1975," said Lou. "Our family gained a new dimension simply because one event cried out for help."

BROCCOLI AND SPEARS

Hospitality sweetens the journey. It's the gift of encouragement and acceptance we offer each other along the way.

While it may begin as a small seed of concern, hospitality has the potential to become a fertile garden that can feed a crowd and satisfy a multitude.

When the fifteen-year-old son of her former classmate was killed in a car accident on his way to school one morning, my friend Ruthmary was among those who agreed to help in the aftermath of the tragedy. The boy's mother, active in their close-knit Louisville community, had been inundated with condolence cards and memorials and was understandably overwhelmed by the task of acknowledging each one. Ruthmary, along with five other women, undertook the onerous job, writing literally thousands of thank you notes for their grieving friend. They couldn't erase her tragic loss, but they could soften the pain with practical gestures of hospitality that gave her time and space to heal.

Every Monday for six weeks, the little group gathered in their friend's home. "We'd take our lunch and visit," said Ruthmary, adding that sometimes their friend joined them, but often just rested in her room, comforted by the murmur of conversation and the presence of people she trusted with her deepest emotions. "Our children were little then and we'd all leave around two or two-thirty to be home when the kids got out of school."

When the thank yous were eventually completed and their grateful friend treated her helpers to lunch, the women agreed that they didn't want to disband. "We had all bonded," said Ruthmary, in ways no one had expected. "We didn't want to let this go." They agreed to meet once each month, gathering for lunch and an informal catch-up to keep the momentum going. In the wake of their decision, however, further losses came their way.

"We began to call ourselves the Grief Group," said Ruthmary. "One of us lost a sister, someone else her mother. A member's brother was killed cutting down a tree in her yard, and the nineteen-year-old daughter of another was paralyzed from the neck down in a serious car crash." The small circle of friends found themselves continuing their tradition of hospitality whenever needs arose. "We'd do anything we could," said Ruthmary—visiting the hospital, bringing food, just listening when someone needed to talk. As time went on, a name change seemed appropriate. "For obvious reasons, nobody wanted to be associated with us," Ruthmary admitted, her sense of humor intact. In the end, a childhood memory of her grandmother became the basis for the group's new title.

"Nana and her friends would catch the bus for downtown Louisville once a week and eat lunch in the Orchid Room of Stewart's Department Store," Ruthmary explained. They wore their best summer dresses, along with white cotton gloves and pearl necklaces. Their feet were snugged into old-fashioned lace-up oxfords, and flowered pillboxes sat on their heads. "They reminded us of something you'd find in the produce department," said Ruthmary. "My sister and I called them the Broccolis."

When Ruthmary's friends heard the story, they clamored to be Broccolis as well, opting for the grammatically incorrect version of the vegetable's plural and carrying on a tradition that so resembled their own. After almost twenty years, the sisterly support of the present-day Broccolis has become a safety net of security and an underpinning of daily life. "Everyone in the group is very spiritual," said Ruthmary. "We have a commitment to pray for each other that's a very strong theme running through our relationships."

There have been changes, of course, alterations and additions that have only enhanced the group's spirit of hospitality. When their children grew up and most of the Broccolis returned to work, the women began meeting for dinner instead of lunch. At Christmas time, their husbands joined them for a holiday feast, and, after several years of getting to know each other, the men decided to start a support group of their own. With a nod to their wives and the asparagus plant that nicely fit the vegetable theme, they dubbed themselves the Spears. Monthly dinners at a local steak house are times for the Spears to sit and talk about their lives, their families, their feelings and concerns. Unlike the usual occasions that bring men together, like sports, card games, or business conferences, the gatherings are an outlet that connects and completes the Spears in an intimate, brotherly way.

The Broccolis and Spears still function separately, but some occasions warrant a joint effort. When one of the Sprouts—their aptly named offspring—becomes engaged, the two groups hold a couples shower at which only one gift is given. "They each get a nativity set," said Ruthmary. "We all agree it's not really about presents, but about teaching the continuity of life. We want our kids to carry on the tradition of strong friendships and strong values that lead to strong marriages."

If one in their group is ill or loses a loved one, the Broccolis and Spears have yet another tradition. "We always send flowers and ask the florists to insert broccoli florets and asparagus spears," Ruthmary added. "Most of the local florists are used to us, but sometimes out-of-towners wonder what in the world we're talking about. It can take a lot of explaining."

Today, I can't look at a cluster of broccoli without thinking of these Louisville ladies. Their quiet presence in a difficult circumstance, their willingness to share the burden of a bereaved parent, drew them into an experience of hospitality they could never have imagined so many years ago. Because they stepped out unselfishly to help, the rewards of hospitality have come back to them a hundred-fold.

PORTABILITY OF HOSPITALITY

Like cuttings from a healthy mother plant, sprigs of hospitality bloom wherever they're planted, quickly adapting themselves to new environments. If I give my daughter some cuttings from the overgrown philodendron on the porch, they grow nicely in her kitchen window or bathroom countertop, taking in light and air as they develop and mature. My daughter can also put the cuttings outside, soaking up the dappled sun and moisture of her backyard garden. New roots and shiny, sometimes variegated leaves are the happy result. Hospitality has the same enduring properties. Because it appears in so many different forms and guises, hospitality clearly packs easily and travels well. The flexibility and portability of this versatile virtue is one of its most attractive aspects.

When my friend Liz was in the early stages of a challenging pregnancy, full course dinners were regularly brought to her home so she could skip kitchen duty until she felt better. When my neighbor Mickey needed a ride to the doctor, another neighbor volunteered to take her. When my brother-in-law Ed was at home recuperating from heart surgery, his buddy Joe appeared at the back door every week with an oversized container of Graeter's ice cream and a grin that said *I care about you, my friend. I hope you'll soon be better.*

Hospitality isn't just about opening the door to people I've invited into my home. It's also about knocking on the door of someone else's house. The portable nature of hospitality makes it a doable, desirable virtue that becomes more and more accessible as it gradually becomes a larger and larger part of our lives. Almost all the stories of hospitality recounted here have involved some element of portability. Let me tell you another, one that hits especially close to home for me.

I met my friend Dianne some years ago, when my son married her beautiful daughter. We shared the usual rounds of bridal showers and wedding festivities, and I found Dianne an easy person to know. She was a single mother who had raised her only child with competence and care. She was also a social worker who could be relied on for high professional standards and compassionate judgment. Her love for her daughter and my son was evident in the way she embraced their new life together and continued to be a significant part of their family.

When Dianne and I became grandparents, we delighted in our mutual blessings. Our granddaughter was a little sunbeam who lit up a room with her laugh. A second pregnancy for my son and his wife meant more joy-filled grandparenting, but this time a larger challenge loomed: twins were on the way.

Twenty-five weeks into the pregnancy, Dianne's strong but small-framed daughter was hospitalized. The threat of premature labor was real and to be avoided at all cost if the twins were to have a chance. At home, my son struggled to keep things together even as his young wife soldiered on in her hospital bed. With a toddler under two and a job to commute to each day, he couldn't manage alone. Dianne, newly retired and all too aware of the dire situation, cut short a Vermont vacation and, dismissing every mother-in-law cliché in the rulebook, became my grateful son's housemate.

"It wasn't sounding good," said Dianne. "I didn't want to take over, but I wanted to be helpful." For the ten weeks that her daughter remained in the hospital, Dianne cared for her young granddaughter after my son left for work. She also cooked and cleaned, did the laundry, and fed the cats. She phoned her daughter each day to gently reassure her that all would be well and saved some extra encouragement for my son, whose stress level had soared to an all-time high. At night, my son took over while Dianne put herself to bed, exhausted. Weekends were breaks, of course. Dianne went home to her condo, about an hour away, and caught up with mail and phone messages. She took time to visit her daughter at the hospital and fed her own cat. Then she turned around and started all over again.

When the twins finally arrived nine weeks later—two healthy boys weighing over five pounds each thanks to the patience and determination of their resolute mother—Dianne realized her task had just begun. A matched set of newborns and a twenty-month-old were far beyond the abilities of two parents, one of whom worked all day to pay the bills. Dianne committed to a long-term stay. This time it not only included pitching in with meals and cleaning, shopping and laundry, but feeding and rocking, soothing and entertaining three little ones who had suddenly become the center of her life. "It was a challenge for everyone, but I never hesitated," Dianne recalled. "Once they said they needed me, that's all it took."

Amazingly, Dianne took the night shift, feeding the babies on demand from one until eight in the morning. Late night television and a heightened sense of responsibility kept her alert. "The twins were so little and there were two of them," she pointed out. "I was afraid to sleep, afraid to even lie down, so I just stayed awake." After being up all night, Dianne stepped into her daytime role, helping her daughter with chores and child care until my son came home and relieved her. Sleep was sandwiched in between five and one, with an hour's rest sometime during the day.

For the first four months of her grandsons' life, Dianne was the extra hand on deck who allowed their little ship to sail efficiently and well. And when she packed up hospitality and carried it from her own heart to the home of her much-loved child, she was also given a renewed sense of purpose and fulfillment. "It felt good that someone still needed and appreciated me," said Dianne. "As tiring as it was, I'd do it again in a second." Watching her energetic grandsons digging in a backyard dirt pile or plundering the pantry for afternoon snacks, Dianne acknowledges her own part in the team effort. "The joy outweighed the pain. Seeing them so happy and healthy makes me think that maybe I contributed a little something to their well-being and the well-being of our family."

Hospitality is a presence. It means being in the *now* with someone else. It's an outpouring of self, linking my innermost need to the needs of others. When I worry that such an effort might be more than I can manage, when I fret that I might not be doing enough, I think of friends who have found themselves instinctively, intuitively practicing hospitality before they were even aware of it. I remember that hospitality already meanders like a peaceful river through the inlets of my life. It's there when I need it, ready to be shared.

H*ospitality is already at work in our lives. Each new day offers fresh opportunities to extend kindness and welcome. Responding instinctively to another's need, we reveal the generous persons God created us to be.*

three

growing

in

hospitality

> Ours is not the task of
> fixing the entire world
> all at once,
>
> but of stretching out to
> mend the part of the world
> that is within our reach.

CLARISSA
PINKOLA-ESTES

One long ago Christmas, when our family was young and the holiday yawned like a gaping chasm of never-ending hours, my husband and I began a tradition of hospitality that we follow to this day. We called it Christmas Soup, an eclectic gathering of neighbors and friends who filled our house and comforted our hearts with seasonal cheer. Over time, Christmas Soup became the lively focus of our family's annual observance.

Our relatives were all firmly planted in the North, while our little band of carpetbaggers had moved south, where my husband's job had led us. We loved our new home, but becoming Georgia peaches meant most holidays were celebrated without benefit of extended family. Memories of Christmas trips to my grandparents' house and festive dinners with a gaggle of relatives lingered like tinsel on an old tree: they were tough to discard and had the staying power of aluminum foil. The first steaming pot of Christmas Soup sprang from my own loneliness and a longing for the trappings of childhood. Far from my parents, siblings, aunts, uncles, and the snowy climate I'd so happily relinquished, I found myself turning sad when yet another Yuletide rolled around.

Our kids were usually up at dawn on Christmas morning. Once they'd torn through their gifts—a feat accomplished in less than ten minutes—it was time for breakfast and on to church. If we were lucky, the neighborhood children got together to show off their new toys or a televised Christmas special entertained us for an hour or two in the afternoon. Most of the time, however, we were in free-fall until dinner, stories, and bedtime rescued us from a very long day.

The notion of Christmas Soup solved my problem. If I rounded up the neighbors, threw them in with a crowd of friends from church and school and served them even the simplest fare, I had the makings of a party. My mother's vegetable beef soup recipe seemed a good bet for hungry guests. I could make gallons beforehand, leave a big pot on the stove, and let folks serve themselves. The sourdough bread I'd recently learned to bake would be a tasty accompaniment. With the sure presence of children, cookies were the perfect finger food.

Our first soup party was a resounding success. Surprisingly, others found themselves with time on their hands and no place to go as Christmas wore on. Friends and neighbors were delighted to share the day, and fellowship hummed through our house like heat through a radiator. Eccentricities were overlooked, idiosyncrasies were tolerated, good cheer prevailed. The kids had fun, too. There were plenty of them, and they snacked and played while parents visited. People came and went, and the day passed in a haze of happy chatter. In the space of an afternoon, Christmas Soup became a tradition we claimed as our own.

Things weren't always perfect at our soup parties. One year, holiday candles dribbled hot wax on our dining room table. A small fire resulted, along with a few moments of pandemonium as we rushed to smother the flames. The fire didn't spread, but it left an interesting scar in the wood that's now a talking point at family gatherings. Some years, neighborhood pets sidled through the front door. We were never sure if the animals were lonesome or hungry, but we bribed them with kid cookies and shooed them out as quickly as we could. Another time, a guest disappeared while the party was in high gear. His four little boys and frantic wife ran around the house searching for their lost patriarch while the rest of us tagged along behind. He was finally discovered in an upstairs bedroom, sleeping soundly, enjoying some needed rest.

Then there was the soup, which required exotic ingredients like leeks and beef bones. Too much barley made the broth gel; too many vegetables clogged it up. Over-salting was a distinct possibility, though I found there could never be enough bay leaves. Every year, I prayed for a cold snap so the unwieldy soup pot could be stored in the carport instead of in our overloaded refrigerator. And when it turned cold, I prayed that the creatures of the night would keep away from the bounty of soup so clearly intended for human consumption. Always, I prayed that the elusive perfection my mother had so effortlessly attained, both in her soup making and her gracious hospitality, would one day be mine.

Looking back, I realize that with every passing year, my confidence grew. The soup got heartier. The bread got tastier. My Christmases were happier. Our modest house swelled with more and more people genuinely enjoying each other's company. In this annual exchange of food and friendship, I discovered the secret to growth in hospitality: practice, practice, practice.

FIVE SIMPLE STEPS

We're all hard-wired with a capacity for goodness. It comes with the package: liver, kidneys, heart, muscle, skin, brains, and the option to be a nice person. I've been given the gift, but I have to untie the shiny ribbon and open the colorful box. I must choose what to do with the potential inside.

Claiming hospitality as an element of personal spirituality means exercising this option for good over and over again. It means practicing with regularity until hospitality becomes a habit of being. What might such practice involve? Five simple steps make hospitality an achievable goal.

1. CULTIVATE A HOSPITABLE HEART

Before I can cultivate a hospitable heart, I must first understand what it means to have one. And the best way to define a hospitable heart is through the example of someone who possessed an uncanny openness and sensitivity to others. Someone who appreciated other people for the gifts they were to him.

When I read about Mychal Judge after the tragedy of September 11, 2001, I recognized in him a spirit of intentional hospitality. The sixty-eight-year-old chaplain for the New York City Fire Department was the first recorded casualty of the infamous day that changed our world. Mychal had rushed to the Twin Towers to offer help where needed and, shortly after giving last rites to an injured firefighter, died in a crush of falling debris. Mychal became famous in death: his funeral was televised, his memorial service drew a packed crowd, and his story was told in countless newspapers and magazines. But Mychal's life, marked with a deep-rooted yet gentle concern for others, is what makes me most appreciate his hospitable heart.

Mychal was a Franciscan friar with a multi-layered ministry that cut a broad swath through the busy metropolis he called home. Born in Brooklyn to Irish immigrants, ordained a priest in 1961, Mychal landed a Manhattan parish assignment in 1986 and six years later became a fire department chaplain. The job was a perfect fit. The firefighting community became Mychal's family, one he served tirelessly. People wondered where his unstoppable energy came from. He turned up in unlikely places at unlikely times. Baptisms and birthdays, bar mitzvahs and anniversaries never went unremembered. Weddings and funerals were always at the top of his list. His phone rang off the hook, and he was faithful about returning messages.

Firefighters were Mychal's first priority, but not to the exclusion of other concerns. He was active in AIDS outreach and regularly engaged the homeless in conversation and prayer. He counseled the addicted and advocated for the outsider. An unconventional crusader, he was as likely to celebrate Mass in Pennsylvania Station or a local firehouse as in his parish church. Mychal was a modern Saint Francis with contemporary clout. His friends ranged from the politically connected to those who made their home on the street. He had time for others because he lived a simple life. Bound by a vow of poverty, he owned little and wanted nothing more. Fueled by an irrepressible desire to offer welcome and acceptance, he was a beloved, familiar figure as he walked the city in his coarse flowing habit and sandaled feet.

"Mychal never rested. He went on and on," recalls Jerry Eifler in his book, *Linger and Be Available*. "He served in whatever fashion he could to make that small corner of the world a better place to live. He was the eyes and ears and hands of God."

Mychal spread himself over New York like peanut butter on a sandwich. He never held back, but channeled his energy into making people feel they were an important part of a whole. The things he did, the words he spoke, the steps he took, led him closer and closer to the ideal of hospitality he so relentlessly pursued. On the day of his death, he was still cultivating a hospitable heart, reaching out to comfort and care for others. While the earth trembled and the city wept, Mychal continued on his sacrificial path. Carried from the ruins by fellow firefighters in a scene likened to a modern *pieta*, Mychal's lifeless body symbolized the depth of his commitment to the hospitality he so unselfishly practiced.

Soon after his death, I came across Mychal's prayer. It's a road map with clear direction and sensible guidance, full of humility and Mychal's characteristic wit. It confirms that hospitality must first begin in the heart before it can be translated into action. The words encourage me to journey with courage on the highway of hospitality and to cultivate a hospitable heart of my own.

> Lord, take me where you want me to go;
> Let me meet who you want me to meet;
> Tell me what you want me to say,
> And keep me out of your way.

2. Emulate Hospitality in Others

My next door neighbor Diane is an avid gardener. On the hottest days, you'll find her digging and planting, arranging and rearranging flowers and greenery in her yard. When it turns cold and the rest of us are huddled by the fire, Diane slips out in a light jacket and gloves to clip and clear and ready the earth for spring planting. Mosquitoes don't bother her, rain makes her sparkle, humidity gives her a rosy glow. Everything Diane puts in the ground not only grows, but thrives. And when she's playing in her garden, refreshed and renewed by sunshine and salty air, Diane thrives too.

Diane's hospitable spirit comes alive in the garden. She's quick to greet neighbors as they stroll around the park in front of her house. Visiting tourists who discover our street off the beaten path of the nearby village are given a warm welcome and friendly chat when they walk by. Diane loves people and people love her. Her garden both expresses and expands her hospitable heart.

When thoughtless drivers and careless cyclists threatened the live oaks and green space in our neighborhood, Diane was quick to act. With a blessing from grateful neighbors, she thinned out the tall green ferns and hardy cast iron plants that had grown to a gracious plenty in her yard. Quietly, without fanfare, she arranged her surplus around the precious oaks, adding more plantings to the corners of the park where vehicles were apt to encroach. In the weeks and months that followed, she watered the plants to ensure a healthy start. She pulled off dead leaves and inspected the foliage for insects and disease. With time and attention, the plants grew tall and strong. They now resemble little green soldiers guarding a treasure, sentries protecting a plot of hallowed ground. Diane's generous effort was an act of hospitality that not only sheltered our neighborhood from damage and despoilment, but also gave us another layer of natural beauty to enjoy.

Diane is modest about her gifts. "I just love to do it," she tells me when I gush over her green thumb. "I'm happiest when I'm digging in the dirt." And when I see the live oaks flourishing in the park, or I'm surprised by an unexpected jar of garden cuttings on my back deck, I'm reminded of Diane's hospitable heart. It not only inspires me, it gives me hope that one person can make a difference.

My friend Martin doesn't know Diane, but he's a kindred spirit. Chivalrous and kind, thoughtful and sensitive, Martin is my idea of a courtly gentleman. He goes out of his way to greet others, to ask about their aches and pains, to inquire after their children and grandchildren. Martin has to be coaxed to talk about himself; he's more concerned with news about *your* life, *your* dreams, *your* troubles and worries. There's a quality about Martin that draws others to him. He exudes an attitude of compassion and empathy few can match, but most can try to emulate.

When my husband and I moved to our island home some years ago, we were grateful that it included a strong faith community. We happily anticipated rolling out of bed on Sundays and making the five-minute drive to our beautiful new church. We had high hopes of making it a central part of our spiritual routine. But as lovely as the church was, with its spectacular skylight, gleaming wood pews, and expansive altar, we were sadly disappointed in the welcome we received there. Fellow parishioners nodded and managed tentative smiles, but few made any effort to get to know us. We became cautious, awaiting some mysterious green light that would allow us to move forward. Martin turned out to be the signal we were looking for.

He was in the choir, and when my husband decided to join the group, it was Martin, a fellow *basso,* who made my spouse feel most at home. Later, when introductions were made, Martin treated me to a courtly bow and kiss on the hand, delivered with unflappable aplomb. *Is this guy for real?* I wondered, sure that such chivalry went out with the Round Table. But as he shot me a grin and a greeting that went right to my heart, I realized his old-fashioned hospitality was exactly what I needed.

Martin became a true and valued friend. He was an irresistible presence, faithful and reliable, optimistic and charming. As time went by and we watched Martin in action, my husband and I agreed that most people at our church weren't initiating conversation because so many were newcomers like ourselves. We began to follow Martin's example and take the lead. We turned up the heat on our hellos, ventured into small talk, glad-handed the quietest folks in the pew. It was a game of sorts: how many people would return our hospitable overtures? How many were just shy, awaiting a friendly greeting, afraid to be too bold? In the end, Martin's code of conduct proved effective.

People responded with gratitude and enthusiasm. Our hospitality might not have flowed as smoothly as Martin's, but we tried to make it as sincere. Today, his habit of hospitality has sunk fledgling roots into my heart. Emulating him has brought me closer to what I believe hospitality ought to be and nearer to the person I'd like to be.

Do you remember Fred Rogers, late host of Public Broadcasting's *Mister Rogers' Neighborhood?* He's long been a hero of mine. When my children were young enough to idolize Fred and his neighborhood of make-believe, it was our custom to gather in the family room and sit goggle-eyed while Fred mesmerized us with song and captured us with kindness. The soft caress of his voice was an injection of comfort into the chaos of the five o'clock hour. He was a welcome and beloved guest in our home.

The remarkable thing about Fred Rogers was that he addressed us as if we were sitting in his living room. He was the perfect host, ever at ease, always ready for a good visit. Slowly, he'd take off his jacket and slip on a cardigan. Unselfconsciously, he'd remove his hard-soled shoes and pull on a pair of sneakers. His tie was left in place, perhaps to remind us that he really was a grownup. Each day, he'd begin his visit with a snappy song he wrote himself: *Let's make the most of this beautiful day. Since we're together, we might as well play.* His words, aimed at his young audience, drew me in too. They were like balm from Gilead, anointing my motherly brow with the oil of acceptance and approval. If I were having a bad day, if the beds weren't yet made and the breakfast dishes not yet cleared from the kitchen table, Fred reminded me I was still okay. I could relax and be myself. He liked me just the way I was.

I knew I could believe Fred. He was honest and earnest, trustworthy and sensitive. An ordained Presbyterian minister with a gift for music, he understood the hidden anxieties of his viewers and realized the significance of their feelings. Consistently respectful, never condescending, Fred Rogers embodied the quintessential hospitable heart. Children intuitively sensed his integrity and interest. He told them things they needed to hear: it's okay to be different; it's all right to be angry or afraid; it's not easy to keep trying, but that's the way we grow.

In *The World According to Mister Rogers*, a posthumous compendium of Fred's thoughts and lyrics, we're reminded that the world is our neighborhood. As members of the human family, "our job in life is to help people realize how rare and valuable each one of us really is, that each of us has something that no one else has—or ever will have— something inside that is unique to all time." Fred Rogers affirmed and validated his audience in a practice of hospitality that reached far beyond his half-hour time slot and the limits of our television screens. Like Martin and Diane, he continues to be an example for me to follow, a paradigm against which I measure my own growth in hospitality. Fred's welcoming smile and sincerity, his unconditional acceptance and understanding, are neighborly qualities I can strive to emulate, no matter how old I grow.

3. EMBRACE THE HOSPITABLE MOMENT

What exactly is a hospitable moment? For me, it's an opportunity to be completely present to another, to be alert and attentive in body, mind, and spirit. Unpredictable, often unplanned, the hospitable moment can pop up when least expected. It's a serendipitous meeting with a friend over coffee or an early morning beach walk with a spouse. It's an e-mail from an old roommate or a long, leisurely catch-up with a grandchild. Circumstances vary, but the likely outcome of a hospitable moment is positive. There's an exchange of spiritual energy that results in a deeper connection. Lives intersect and harmony prevails.

When I was pregnant with our first child, I spent a long, hot summer in our one-bedroom apartment fighting boredom and nausea while the rest of the world went on without me. One sultry afternoon, as I tried to plan a dinner my stomach could survive and my husband would enjoy, I heard a tentative knock on our old metal door. Peeking through its ancient peephole, I spied a young woman about my own age with a heavy briefcase and forced smile. "I just want a minute of your time," she told me unconvincingly.

Inside, I saw that the saleslady who stood before me was even more pregnant than I. With a thin film of sweat on her forehead and the look of a desperate housewife on her face, she was, I thought, badly in need of a chair and a glass of cold tea. I presented her with both and, as she settled in, watched as she opened a thick volume of Collier's Encyclopedia and flipped the pages in my direction. I was, I realized, quite trapped, stuck in my chair, listening politely as my visitor huffed and puffed her way through a scripted presentation. It was the sixties version of a telemarketing spiel, a living phone call I couldn't cut off.

"A set of these encyclopedias would be just right for that baby you're expecting," she said with a pasted grin on her face. "What a great resource they'll be when he's in school!" My weary guest neglected to mention that the books would be out of date by the time our little one reached first grade. Or that by high school they'd be posted on the Internet and easily accessed at home or in class. For my part, I forgot that funds were scant and our budget was tight. Propelled by a desire to do the very best for my unborn child and the empathy I felt for this fellow mother-to-be, I poured another glass of iced tea and signed on the dotted line.

"We bought what?" my husband later asked when I told him our child was now ready for scholarly pursuits and we'd be making monthly payments until the baby finished college. His eyes widened and his lips closed tightly around the words he so kindly left unsaid as I sputtered through an explanation, trying to convince him—and myself—of the soundness of our purchase. In the end, we agreed that the books couldn't hurt and might help.

Over the years, we hauled those unwieldy tomes up and down the East Coast, moving from place to place with our young family. Our kids used the encyclopedias for book reports and science projects, usually requiring updates from more recent publications in the library or online. The infamous books were a considerable annoyance and a running joke between my husband and me. In retrospect, we laughed at ourselves and our youthful naiveté. I learned from the experience and no longer flew by the seat of my pants when it came to financial decisions. But every time I picked up one of the black-bound, red-striped volumes that nestled in our creaky pine bookcase, I flashed back to that tired, pregnant woman who had spent a hot August afternoon with me.

I regretted buying the books. I regretted the money lost and the dated material. I even regretted the loss of time that had made that night's dinner a hurried, uninspired affair. But I had no regrets about embracing what was, for me, a hospitable moment. That saleswoman came to my door, and I invited her to rest her hands and her feet, to refresh herself at my table. I listened as she did her job, working hard to put a few extra pennies in her pocket. She was a fellow traveler and, like me, full of new life. I don't count myself an especially generous type, but on that day, some grace enabled me to pull out the stops and make her welcome. Without thinking, I responded. And, when I did, she responded too. I never saw her again, but I will always remember her because of the hospitable moment we shared.

Time has passed and the children for whom the books were purchased are now parents themselves. I am blessed with a wagonload of grandchildren and, as a grandparent, have discovered that hospitable moments erupt whenever I'm with these delightful companions of my later years. We conduct tea parties and dress Barbie dolls. We play board games at the kitchen table and dance around the living room to catchy music. We swing and slide and climb in the park and wade in their backyard pools. Although I may not do *everything* my grandchildren want me to do, I'm keenly aware that these little people won't always be so available and enthusiastic. Change is inevitable. Adolescence and adulthood are just around the corner. The moments of intimacy I share with my young grandchildren, like the tender moments I spent with their parents, are times that will not come again. If I'm open to the gift of the present, ready to embrace the hospitable moments that fall in my lap like petals from a flower, I'll have no regrets.

One long weekend in early summer, when my husband and I were babysitting for three of our grandchildren, we stayed one step ahead of chaos by sticking to a sensible routine. During the day, we wore the kids down with outdoor activities. We made sure they rested after lunch and added more exercise to their afternoons. We fed them healthy meals and read them favorite stories. We tried to get their little minds off the fact that their parents had vanished into thin air.

Things were going well until a hot June day spawned a series of wild evening storms. Claps of thunder rumbled in the distance. Flashes of lightning warned that drama was headed our way. Fortunately, we'd already had dinner and the kids were pajama-clad and freshly diapered. A promised pre-bedtime movie had just begun when a noisy wind started rattling the house. My husband shut down the television, and I turned off the air conditioner; the house lights were flashing and we didn't want to blow any major electrical fuses. The kids scrambled onto the couch and snuggled in around us. With pillows and blankets, stuffed animals and scrubbed faces, we had an instant pajama party.

Every time the thunder rolled, the children made their own sound effects. *Ooooh! Wwoww! Mmm-mi! Paa-pa!* Their little eyes twinkled with a delicious combination of fear and excitement. They huddled like kittens under the cellar steps. When a pillar of light and noise exploded in the back yard, we all jumped two feet off the sofa. A tall pine had definitely gone down, we decided, grateful it hadn't hit the house. The sky continued to darken. Rain started falling—hard, then harder—as we alternated listening with sucking in our breath. To pass the time, we sang songs and read stories, but mostly we just held on to each other, rocking together in our upholstered ark while the storm beat on the doors and windows.

In the time that the storm possessed us, we were totally present to each other. We had nothing to do but to sit on the couch and be together. In just twenty minutes of meteorological madness, grandparents and grandchildren were closer than we'd ever been, comforted by the sound of each other's breathing, the touch of each other's skin. When the storm passed, our moment of intimacy was integrated into our family history. We'd weathered a storm that had entertained and delighted us, even as it surprised and alarmed us at the same time. Our love for each other was more deeply rooted because we had shared a hospitable moment.

4. ENJOY SOLITUDE

Often, a hospitable interlude with someone else is easier to arrange than a similar window of opportunity with myself. Seizing a moment of solitude for self-care and nurturing can be challenging, especially when other obligations demand so much time and energy. Yet, if I'm serious about growing in hospitality, if I truly aspire to become proficient at this virtue, I must first, last, and always extend hospitality to myself. If I don't, if I put myself last on the list and ignore what so clearly is a right and privilege, my supply of hospitality, however well intentioned, will quickly dry up and float away on the next breeze. I can't give what I don't have.

"You cannot really love your neighbor unless you love yourself first," counseled Catherine de Hueck Doherty, the Russian baroness who founded Madonna House Apostolate in Combermere, Ontario, and popularized solitary retreats of inner stillness and prayerful listening. After spending time in solitude, Catherine writes in her book *Poustinia*, our spiritual awareness is heightened and our presence to others takes on richer meanings. Confronting our own deepest self allows us "to bring (God) to the street, the party, the meeting, in a very special and powerful way." We become carriers of a silent *poustinia*—a quiet desert where God abides—within ourselves.

My cousin Chris, a professional designer with a host of celebrity clients and a score of interior decorating books to her credit, is fluent in the language of hospitality. Growing up in a family of eleven, she learned the basics of the virtue early on and has translated her love of home and hearth into a flourishing business. "Keep it simple, but make it special," Chris is apt to suggest. "Turn the ordinary into the extraordinary" with candlelight dinners, celebration breakfasts, and home accents that satisfy all five senses. But while Chris encourages people to cherish a home whose warmth and charm draws others close, she's keenly aware of the need for solitary space as well.

"When my younger sister died, I didn't have a place to mourn her," she recalled. The tragic loss became an impetus for action. Not long after her sister's death, Chris converted a small bedroom into a private study and sitting area, carving out a room of her own that allowed her space to grieve. "If you don't take care of yourself first, you can't give out to others without anger and resentment. You can't experience joy," she believes. "We must find the time to feed our own souls, to create an environment of the spirit. It's not about selfishness. It's about nurturing ourselves."

Camden, my friend and yoga instructor, encourages the same kind of inner attentiveness. "Spend time with yourself," she advises. "Discover what you need today. Don't judge. Surrender, breathe, observe." Teaching a centuries-old discipline that links mind and body through the spirit of the breath, Camden knows hospitality can either hold us back or propel us forward. Her example teaches me that maintaining an open, receptive attitude—accepting myself warts and all—invariably leads to acceptance of others. When I treat myself with the gentle compassion I'd offer a close friend or even a stranger, I satisfy needs deep within me. I set boundaries and honor my feelings. I respect my body and my mind. By embracing the solitary moment, I make room for contemplation and recreation, for prayer and daydreaming. I come to know the person I truly am, as well as the person I'd like to be.

How do *you* spend time with yourself? My friend Stella loves to garden. Anne likes to paint. My neighbor Randy would rather fish than eat, while Marilyn finds delight in the creation of intricate pottery designs. Jim's an accomplished woodworker who's constructed a small but seaworthy boat. Alicia is a talented cook whose family and friends enjoy the delicious results of her kitchen magic. As for me, I like to read, to work crossword puzzles, to walk to the ocean in the early morning. I love old movies with happy endings and offbeat novels with a sense of humor. Sometimes, when sleep eludes me, I sit on my porch and watch the dawning light wrap itself around the trees and houses of our neighborhood. If I'm up late at night, I like to peer at the moon shining through the back window.

We can all find ways to refresh and renew ourselves by embracing hospitable moments spent in our own good company. It doesn't matter what we do with our time alone. What's important is wresting it out of our busy schedules and using it to heal and recharge. If we hope to share hospitality with others, we must replenish our personal supply.

5. SEEK THE GRACE OF HOSPITALITY

Happily, hospitality is not an elusive, pie in the sky virtue. It's an interactive, hands-on element of spirituality, accessible to anyone who takes time to cultivate it, to give it light and space to grow. But like any virtue, hospitality needs more than just a simple human effort if it's to plant its roots deeply and firmly in my life. It requires an infusion of God's grace if it's to become more than just a breezy social distraction or an occasional lighthearted evening spent in the company of familiar faces.

"Hospitality is a talent and a gift," says my friend Sharon, whose home and heart are ever open to family, friends, and the strangers she meets along the way. For Sharon and her husband Jim, God is at work in the hospitality they practice. Hospitality is a treasure they're meant to share. As they understand it, the gift of hospitality has been given to them for the benefit of others and the enhancement of their own personal growth.

When a steady stream of company filters through my front door, when the refrigerator gasps in exhaustion from too many meals in too few days, and my body shuts down from chasing grandchildren around the park, I realize I can't make hospitality happen on my own. I have to seek spiritual help, to pray that God will bless the baby steps I take and give me strength to persevere when hospitality isn't easy.

While I may endeavor to cultivate a hospitable heart, emulate hospitality in others, embrace moments of hospitality, and enjoy the hospitality of personal time and space, I can't neglect my need for the *grace* of hospitality. I must humbly ask God to let hospitality grow beyond and in spite of my human faults and imperfections, my impatience and ego. When I seek the grace of hospitality, I count on God to transform my simple strivings into marvelous deeds and wonderful outcomes.

H*ospitality is an accessible virtue, meant to be studied and practiced in the school of real people and everyday events. The lessons of hospitality are best learned when we're alert to possibilities and generous enough to embrace them. Growth is assured when hospitality becomes a spiritual priority.*

four

hospitality

is part of

our tradition

> Hospitality, like every-
> thing else, has been
> commercialized.
>
> So hospitality, like
> everything else, must now
> be idealized.

PETER MAURIN

I was living in Atlanta when Mother Teresa came to town. The diminutive nun with a face like a hazelnut was opening a hospice for women with AIDS, and it was my job to write about the visit for a local newspaper. The legendary lady of the poor was so small and frail I wanted to put my arms around her and give her a gentle hug.

"She's just like your grandma," my friends Henry and Mary had told me years earlier. Together they'd traveled to India and volunteered at some of the facilities Mother Teresa had opened there. Henry, our children's pediatrician, and his wife, Mary, a nurse, found Mother Teresa approachable and warm, surprisingly easy to be with. During her Atlanta visit, I didn't have the opportunity to engage Mother in conversation or work side by side with her as my friends had done, but I sat close enough to observe her tranquil manner, her focused gaze and humble garb.

She wore what looked like a linen dishtowel on her head and her little body was crinkled with age and labor. Her gnarled feet rested in a pair of worn leather sandals. Surrounded by broad-shouldered bodyguards and police who'd come from as far away as New England to secure her safety, she appeared stooped and frail. Her appearance, however, belied the power of her message. This was a person who knew her mind and spoke it convincingly. Fueled by a tradition of faith-based hospitality, she stood on its promises like a queen on a throne. She was a Roman Catholic nun, at one with all those whose spiritual beliefs have inspired works greater than themselves.

"I remember once I picked up this man from the street," Mother Teresa told the teeming congregation that had gathered in Atlanta's historic Sacred Heart Church. "He was full of worms, and I took him to our home." When he arrived, she related, the man said he'd lived like an animal on the streets, but was going to die like an angel. With a smile lighting her wizened countenance at the memory of the rescue, Mother Teresa noted that caring for others has its own unique rewards because it reflects the love of a compassionate God. "This is the joy of serving. This is what Jesus said: 'Whatever you do to the least, you do to me.'"'

Mother Teresa's overriding focus was hospitality to those desperately in need of it. Under her leadership, hospitals, schools, orphanages, leper colonies, and hospices were built and staffed by the order she founded, the Missionaries of Charity. Unwanted children, ailing bodies riddled with disease, people left to die in the street were lifted up, taken in, and given a place of safety and refuge. "To be unwanted and unloved, a throwaway of society—that is the greatest disease today," Mother Teresa believed. "The only cure is willing hands to serve and hearts to go on loving them." Though she didn't seek celebrity, the world revered and honored her. She accepted the 1979 Nobel Peace Prize in the name of the poor she so faithfully tended.

When people asked Mother Teresa how they could help relieve pandemic poverty and universal suffering, she counseled that hospitality began within their own families and neighborhoods. Itinerant students, transient volunteers, and starry-eyed idealists eager to change the world were all directed back to their center. "Love begins by taking care of the closest ones, the ones at home," Mother Teresa often said. She believed poverty wasn't just about a lack of bread, but was as near as the husband, wife, child, parent, or neighbor who feels isolated and alone. Global transformation, in her opinion, starts with care of the least important, least noticed, least loved in our own households and communities.

Mother Teresa died in 1997. The little nun with the giant heart was beatified in 2003 and is well on her way to sainthood. Like so many others, I canonized her a long time ago, and being in close physical proximity to *one* living saint would have been enough for me. But I was blessed by the presence of another.

My husband and I met as students in Italy in the mid-sixties and returned to Rome for our twentieth wedding anniversary. While there, we were given tickets to a papal liturgy by a kindly nun we'd met in Saint Peter's Square. The Mass was scheduled for students and educators, and the gracious lady insisted we take her extra tickets even though our student days were long past. It was, she said, an anniversary gift.

We easily blended into the crowded basilica. It wasn't our first visit to Saint Peter's, but the pope had a new face. In 1986, John Paul II, the Polish cardinal whose election broke the long-standing tradition of Italian popes, was in remarkably sound health. He radiated a physical and spiritual vitality that was irresistible to the young, while his openness and good humor attracted people of all ages. The liturgy that day was an enthusiastic celebration of hope and encouragement. At the end of Mass, John Paul strolled down the main nave, stopping to greet people who strained to see and touch him. At one point in the leisurely recessional, he spied a visitor who warranted special notice. A young man with Down's syndrome, in the outermost seat of a pew halfway up the aisle, drew the pope's attention above all others. My own seat was perfectly angled for a view of their meeting. They embraced warmly. The pope looked affectionately into the man's eyes and slowly blessed him with a sign of the cross.

After Pope John Paul II died in 2005, the Catholic Church placed him on the fast track to official sanctity. I never questioned the decision. I had sensed the measure of the man when I saw him single out and warmly welcome the handicapped student who was with us in St. Peter's twenty-odd years ago. Like Mother Teresa, John Paul was firmly rooted in a tradition of hospitality that was a natural expression of his beliefs. He lived out this tradition in an extraordinary way over the course of his papacy, traveling the world with a message of inclusion and affirmation. His desire for religious unity, respect for human rights, and recognition of the dignity of the human person propelled him to extend and receive hospitality from people of all faiths, in all corners of the earth. His vision of global solidarity was just a larger version of the brief encounter I was privileged to witness on my unforgettable anniversary trip.

HALLMARK OF CHRISTIANITY

"Hospitality is more about open hearts than open doors," my friend John believes. A Catholic priest who emigrated from Ireland to serve the mission territory of the southern United States, John's understanding of hospitality is borne of personal experience. He was himself a stranger in a foreign land obliged to depend on the goodwill of others.

"Ireland was the only place I had really known," he told me. Money was tight in post-war Europe and travel was a luxury John's family couldn't afford. When he left his home in Cork in 1969 at the age of twenty-four, he'd only been as far as England. Coming to the States was an act of faith.

"The thing that helped me most was the hospitality that was extended to me," said John. The overwhelming acceptance he received made a critical difference in his adjustment to a new way of life. "You take a risk when you're hospitable to a stranger," he knew, yet found himself treated like a friend from the first moment. Posted to a busy church in Augusta, Georgia, he was quickly immersed in the life of the community. One of his earliest memories is of accompanying two parishioners to a football game at their alma mater. "We drove up to Athens in a huge Cadillac to see the University of Georgia play," he said with a grin. "After the game, I learned all about tailgating."

Despite his status as the new guy in town, John was invited into people's homes and into their lives. "They accepted me totally. There were no conditions. I was part of their parish, but became part of their families as well." Decades later, John is still at home in the South. He pastors the large coastal parish I attend and is now an administrator of the diocese he so generously pledged to serve almost forty years ago. In an age of alarm systems, peepholes and gated communities, John feels, the world needs hospitality more than ever.

"Hospitality is a hallmark of a follower of Christ," he reminds his congregation. "What we're called to do as hospitable people is at the very heart of the Gospel message. To welcome a stranger is to welcome Christ himself." John's Celtic sense of welcome rings true, echoed in countless communities of hospitality operating today in the name of a compassionate God. Hospitality is a fundamental human attribute, but when it is planted firmly in the Christian tradition, it graduates to the next level. It becomes a sacrament of the everyday, a sacred trust, a blessed obligation.

MONASTIC ROOTS

When our children were young, our family lived not far from the Abbey of Our Lady of the Holy Spirit in Conyers, Georgia. One of our favorite weekend outings was a forty-minute trip to this large tract of Trappist property east of Atlanta. We'd pack a picnic, hustle the kids in the car and head for the monastery. Once off the interstate, we found the roads rough and often unmarked. Before subdivisions and malls crowded Rockdale County's rural farms and homes, the site was a hidden treasure. Directions were required, and even then, visitors depended on primitive, hand-lettered signs placed at strategic intersections and on the sides of the road to reach their destination. Often, we retraced our steps to get back on track.

But once we arrived, the sprawling grounds of Holy Spirit held delightful discoveries. There was the abbey church, built by the monks themselves in the early 1950s, some years after the monastery's founding in 1944. Our kids loved to climb the narrow staircase that led to the choir loft and view the beautiful sanctuary below. Not far from the church, the bookstore beckoned. After a cordial chat with Brother Pius, our usual greeter, we'd peruse a vast selection of books and religious goods, including original sand castings and stained glass created by the monks. Beyond the bookstore, there was a lush greenhouse full of chubby succulents and graceful bonsai. We never left without some exotic plants and a few loaves of the monastery's delicious brown bread.

The lake and picnic area were within walking distance of the bookstore, in the midst of a shady pine grove. No matter what we brought for lunch, the resident swans were always interested. Sometimes they'd pretend to ignore us and wait for crumbs. If they were cranky, they'd stalk and hiss like rubber-necked bullies. After placating the swans with bread crusts, we'd amble over to a fenced area where the remnants of Flannery O'Connor's flock of peacocks then lived. Given to the monastery during the author's final battle with lupus, they were a reminder of what Mary Flannery called her passion for chickens, a quest that had "ended with peacocks," according to her essay, *The King of the Birds*. Often, one of the peacocks would fan his tail and strut around the pen. Like Ms. O'Connor, we'd watch the display, "always with the same awe," no matter how many times we'd seen it before.

The hours our family spent at the monastery are some of the happiest in my memory. Holy Spirit was a safe and restful place, full of serenity and calm. It exuded an unspoken hospitality that colored our every visit. There weren't many places we could take four noisy, energetic children and expect an unconditional welcome. But at the monastery, our kids felt at home, just as my husband and I did. On our walks through the grounds, we encountered monks busy at their chores who were never too preoccupied to chat, to engage the children, to inquire about our interests and concerns. The freedom we experienced at the monastery was a blessing that flowed from a community steeped in the art and practice of hospitality.

RULE OF SAINT BENEDICT

Our Lady of the Holy Spirit monastery continues to thrive today. People still picnic by the lake and seek solitude in the retreat house. Daily Mass and liturgy of the hours are open to the public in the abbey church. *Plein air* painters have joined the visitors' ranks, and the monastery's well-stocked food pantry now serves the hungry in five surrounding counties.

These hospitable monks take their cue from the Rule of Saint Benedict, a sixth-century code of conduct written for ordinary people desiring to live in conscious contact with their God. Benedict, born into Italian nobility but led to a life of poverty and prayer, directed his writings to spiritual seekers. Today his Rule, a masterful balance of work and prayer, has become the foundation for Western monasticism and a source of inspiration for countless lay people who rely on its simple wisdom for daily direction.

Benedict was explicit in his admonition to practice hospitality. "Let all guests who arrive be received like Christ," he wrote in chapter fifty-three of the Rule. "And to all let due honor be shown. . . . As soon as a guest is announced . . . let the Superior or the brethren meet him with all charitable service. . . . In the reception of the poor and of pilgrims the greatest care and solicitude should be shown, because it is especially in them that Christ is received."

For Benedict, hospitality was a priority. Abbots were advised to break their fasts and dine with hungry guests. Visitors had their feet washed, were prayed with, fed, and lodged in comfortable quarters. The basis of this attitude was the belief that God himself is present in the person of the stranger. "In the salutation of all guests, whether arriving or departing, let all humility be shown," states the Rule. "Let the head be bowed or the whole body prostrated on the ground in adoration of Christ, who indeed is received in their persons. "

No doubt it wasn't always convenient for the community to be interrupted by guests. No doubt some guests were more appealing than others, more appreciative of the monks' efforts. But Benedict's clarity brooks no protest: *No whining; no complaints. Drop what you're doing and put a smile on your face. This tired, disheveled, hungry traveler needs a break, and you're going to give it to him.* Eventually, the spirit of Benedict's Rule penetrated not only monastic communities, but all of Christendom. Today, the guest house remains a significant part of abbey life, an outward sign of commitment to the world beyond monastery walls. In the homes of those who believe, as Benedict did, that Christ comes in the guise of a visitor, the door of welcome is always open.

HOUSE OF HOSPITALITY

When my youngest daughter entered school, I found a little time for volunteering. I squeezed it in between school drop-offs and pickups, soccer practices and grocery shopping. Once a week I headed to a midtown soup kitchen to help prepare and serve lunches for indigent and homeless people. At Atlanta's Open Door Community, I discovered a place where my gifts for chopping and cleaning vegetables, making sandwiches and setting a table could be put to good use.

While everyone who visited Open Door needed help, their backgrounds were often quite different. Some had recently lost a job; others were chronically unemployed. Some suffered from the disease of alcoholism; others were mentally compromised because of youthful drug abuse. Some smelled of soap and after-shave; others hadn't bathed in a week. Women and children came, too. They were part of a whole, a stream of humanity that was easy to overlook in a city that had bigger fish to fry.

Open Door was aptly named. An active community of permanent staff, volunteers, and resident guests, it was also a focal point for compassionate outreach. Situated on a main thoroughfare in an accessible metro location, Open Door had been a stately, well-kept home before time and neglect took its toll. With some serious cleaning and remodeling, however, the residence acquired a fresh look and a renewed purpose. Its front door was open to receive the needy. Its back yard was restful green space for weary feet. Its wide front porch was shelter on a steamy summer afternoon or a chilly winter morning.

Open Door was a true soup kitchen: a daily lunch of soup was served, along with sandwiches, tea, and dessert if it was available. Depending on the supplies at hand and the skills of the day's soup maker, the fare would range from a hearty vegetable medley to a tummy-soothing chicken noodle. If the government's surplus cheddar arrived, cheese sandwiches were offered. If a local restaurant or convention center donated leftover meats, ham or chicken was tucked in with the cheese. When everything ran out, peanut butter and jelly was a reliable back up, though objections were occasionally raised. *Hey, he's got cheese—where's mine? I thought there was supposed to be meat in this soup! How come there aren't seconds on dessert today?*

I once asked a seasoned volunteer why guests complained about the menu when their resources were clearly limited and the food they were eating was freely given. I was told that Open Door's clientele had so little control over their lives that they exercised their few options in any small way they could. Inappropriate behavior was never excused at Open Door, but tolerance and patience were as much a part of the luncheon experience as soup and sandwiches.

Practicality also prevailed. Because bare necessities are luxuries to most homeless folks, first floor showers and telephones were made available on certain days of the week. A clothes closet was always stocked with usable donations and transit tokens were routinely given to those requiring transportation. Job opportunities, addiction counseling, and spiritual guidance rounded out the nourishing fare Open Door served to people hungry for human kindness.

CATHOLIC WORKER MOVEMENT

The hospitality I happily shared at Open Door had its roots in the Catholic Worker Movement. Though Open Door was begun and is still ably managed by people of the Presbyterian faith, it's linked to an international network of nearly two hundred Catholic Worker communities steadfastly committed to prayer, nonviolence, voluntary poverty, and hospitality. In targeting injustice, war, racism, and violence in all forms, today's Catholic Workers stand on the broad shoulders of Dorothy Day and Peter Maurin, who founded the movement at the height of the Depression.

Dorothy, a single mother and a convert to Catholicism, had a background in journalism and social activism. Peter, a French peasant and teacher, was committed to a revision of the current social order. Their fortuitous meeting in New York in 1932 spawned a spiritual partnership based on a shared belief in the dignity of the human person. It resulted in the publication of *The Catholic Worker* newspaper, which continues in print today, and the steady growth of a movement that fostered justice and empowerment for society's least-valued members.

James Allaire and Rosemary Broughton, authors of *Praying with Dorothy Day*, note that the Catholic Worker vision of social and personal transformation was enthusiastically received, especially because it emerged as an acceptable alternative at a time when many believed only radical Communism addressed the needs of the masses. Twenty-first century Catholic Worker communities continue to attest to the enduring legacy of a mission so clearly identified by Dorothy and Peter.

In Houston, Texas, Casa Juan Diego serves immigrants and refugees in multiple houses of hospitality within the city. A women's house accommodates up to fifty females, with a focus on pregnant and battered women and their children. A men's house holds sixty, while a separate facility shelters sick or recovering men. Additionally, the casa offers English classes, food and clothing, medical, dental, and social services to those needing help.

In Sheep Ranch, California, a Catholic Worker farm sits on part of an eighty-acre land trust in the foothills of the Sierra Nevada Mountains. Workers founded and now oversee the trust, promoting proper stewardship of the land and its irreplaceable resources. They also operate a retreat facility for people with AIDS and their caregivers, as well as a summer program for disabled adults.

In Hamburg, Germany, the *Brot und Rosen* community campaigns against nuclear proliferation and waste in a spirit of environmental hospitality. In Notre Dame, Indiana, the Holy Family Catholic Worker House welcomes homeless families who need help getting back on their feet. In Oklahoma City, Oklahoma, the Oscar Romero Catholic Worker House delivers weekly bags of groceries to needy people unable to get to the local food bank. In Boston, Massachusetts, Haley House serves over thirty-five thousand meals a year to the homeless and elderly, publishes an alternative magazine, and operates a bakery café that includes training for those transitioning into the job market.

Like all contemporary Catholic Worker communities, Samaritan House in Vancouver, Canada, holds itself to strict standards of hospitality. Its edifying credo is faithful to the ideals of the early founders and could be the motto to which all Worker houses subscribe: *We believe in peace and justice. We believe in the fellowship of all humanity. We believe in compassion. We believe in speaking out to cajole, compel, inspire, and admonish.*

In 1983, I visited the Catholic Worker houses in New York City, where Dorothy and Peter had begun their work of hospitality. Both houses were full of people who made me, a stranger, feel at home. Both houses had small gardens, islands of quiet that were respites from the hectic pace of the bustling city just outside the door. Both had a tangible aura of peace that was relaxing and reassuring, an aura that remained with me even after I returned home.

At Saint Joseph House, on East First Street in lower Manhattan, I helped make sandwiches to accompany the day's soup. The savory brew was simmering in the largest metal pot I'd ever encountered, stirred by a volunteer with a regulation sized boat oar. A short walk away, at Maryhouse, former site of the Third Street Music School, I explored the women's residence. It was, I was told, an invaluable resource, especially during harsh New York winters when homeless women were particularly vulnerable.

Volunteers acknowledged that life in a Catholic Worker house wasn't paradisiacal. Personalities clashed; people disagreed; needs weren't always met. But despite the inevitability and persistence of human foibles, living in a community of intentional hospitality allowed these individuals to operate at a higher level. It was a life they'd chosen because it resonated as a sound choice for a person of faith.

SOARING WITH EAGLES

Commitment and purpose are what led Eddie Staub to found Eagle Ranch over twenty years ago. The congenial six-footer with a soft Alabama drawl had an idyllic childhood and an education that had prepared him well for a promising future in teaching and coaching. But he bypassed the predictable path for rising stars and chose instead to build a place in the foothills of the Appalachians where troubled children could heal and grow.

Eddie's motto, a handwritten note to himself that's now framed and hangs in Eagle Ranch's administration building, was a guiding light, especially in the early days when money was tight and prospects bleak: *Attempt something so great for God that it's doomed to failure unless God be in it.* Though the ranch thrives today, serving more than fifty boys and girls in group homes staffed with caring house parents, circumstances weren't always so bright.

In his compelling history of the ranch, *On Eagle's Wings,* John Vardeman recounts Eddie's conversation with a potential supporter. "I'm twenty-seven years old, and all I have is a dream to give little boys a home," said the young idealist. Eddie boldly stated his plight: no money, no land, no local contacts to open doors for him. Before his quest was over, he was down to his last fifty dollars and had been reduced to a diet of cheese, crackers, and milk. Hope was running out when an unexpected infusion of $10,000 in foundation monies started Eagle Ranch down the road to success. As moral and financial support grew, Eddie acquired a 180-acre spread on north Georgia's Chestnut Mountain that came with a lake perfectly suited for fishing, boating, and swimming. Volunteer groups from local churches and civic groups helped clear land, plant shrubs and paint new buildings. The first boys' residence was built, eventually followed by seven more group homes. Today, horses run free in wide-open pastures. Athletic fields are manicured for steady use. Bass, blue gill and catfish swim idly in the lake. The ranch boasts an on-site school, a counseling program run by licensed professionals, and a growing number of well-adjusted graduates who have moved on to lead productive lives. Over five hundred children aged six through eighteen have passed through the gates of Eagle Ranch.

I met Eddie when Eagle Ranch was just getting off the ground. Tony and Trisha, friends from my church, were among the first houseparents, and I was treated to an insider's look at the operation. Before my visit, I'd had my doubts about Eddie Staub. Frankly, he sounded too good to be true. I expected a Bible-thumping egotist with grandiose plans guaranteed to make himself a headliner. Early on, CNN news had called Eagle Ranch "the miracle on Chestnut Mountain," and I was anticipating hype and hoopla. I dined instead on humble pie.

Eddie was as eager and enthusiastic as a kid at his first baseball game. He graciously received me and shared his personal story as well as the history of the ranch. If I'd had any doubts, they quickly dissolved in the explosion of sunlight that radiated from Eddie's honest face. He was smart, sincere, and driven by an understanding of hospitality I had yet to learn. His goal for the children who came to Eagle Ranch was to help them heal and, ultimately, to reunite them with their families of origin. Through family weekends, individual and family-centered counseling, plus hard work all around, the latter goal was often achieved. Children who lived at Eagle Ranch had deep emotional scars—problems that couldn't be solved without a change of environment and a structured lifestyle. Eagle Ranch was a home away from home, a healthy setting where study, outdoor activity, and reflection fostered personal freedom and self-control.

"We haven't done a whole lot," my friend Tony said of his houseparenting duties at Faith House, one of the first residences built on ranch grounds. Of course, I knew better. Tony's modesty was commendable but the obvious sacrifice he and his wife, Trisha, made had been significant. They'd uprooted themselves from longstanding jobs and a traditional suburban neighborhood and replanted their young family in an unfamiliar place where daily life took on the dynamics of a boarding house. It would all have been impossible without an underlying belief that the hospitality offered at Eagle Ranch reflected a larger reality. "The secret of our success is the power of God," Tony said. He and Trisha rested in the knowledge that they'd been called to a life of faith, not results. They'd been asked to love these children unconditionally, doing their best to put their own needs and wants on the back burner.

Some days were harder than others, they admitted. Corralling a house full of busy boys could be rough going, especially when their charges were working out the personal issues that had brought them to Eagle Ranch. The rewards, however, usually outweighed the challenges. Their call to a ministry of hospitality was often blessed with surprising results.

One Holy Thursday, my friends ended their evening devotional with a foot-washing ceremony. Tony scrubbed the feet of their seven "adopted" sons and the couple's own two children, while Trisha followed up with individual foot massages and toenail trimming. They hoped the youngsters would enjoy the special attention and at the same time understand the importance of serving others. By the following Sunday, their hopes had been realized. When the Faith House family gathered at a local restaurant for Easter dinner, the children were prepared. As the last of their meal was cleared away, the kids brought out water and towels and proceeded to wash the feet of their startled but very grateful house parents.

"[T]hose who wait for the Lord shall renew their strength, they shall mount up with wings like eagles, they shall run and not be weary, they shall walk and not faint" (Is 40:31) is the scriptural promise the ranch has claimed for its own. As Eagle Ranch continues its tradition of hospitality to children once too weary to run, my friends see faithfulness rewarded and promises fulfilled.

CREATING TRADITIONS

I was lucky enough to grow up in a family where hospitality was a valued commodity. People weren't turned away. Food was shared, extra beds were available, understanding ears were ready to listen. When my mother lined up my younger brothers for monthly haircuts, their buddies got haircuts too. When my father took the family for weekend boat rides, friends were always on board. Holidays were times to visit and be visited. Samplings from my mother's kitchen were the best gifts anyone could hope to receive. Our family observed a tradition of hospitality inspired by the loving hearts of my generous parents.

Growing up in a small town where everyone's business was grist for gossip, I learned early on that silence often meant survival. Still in grade school when a young, unmarried member of our church became pregnant, I sensed it was yet another matter to be discreetly ignored. To confront such a situation was to acknowledge it, to make it real, to risk embarrassing the family and mother-to-be. In the minds of most, kindness took the form of avoiding the subject, looking the other way, pretending it didn't happen, and letting things unfold as they naturally would.

The young woman in question was a daughter of family friends who themselves were well-known in our community. *Mumble, mumble. Hush, hush.* Tongues might wag, but not loudly enough to be heard by neighbors. At our house, the subject of an unmarried mother didn't surface at the dinner table. We observed the usual rules about sidestepping fiery topics and stuck to mundane reports about the torments we suffered at the hands of our teachers that day. As the oldest, however, I was privy to activities behind the scenes. My mother, I discovered, had been mulling things over and took me into her confidence.

"This baby must be welcomed," she firmly believed. "This baby's mother needs to be reassured, to know she's loved and supported by her friends." While I nodded my head, Mom brought out a yellow crib blanket and an embroidered sweater set, complete with tiny booties she'd purchased at a local department store. Sadly, there would be no baby showers, she explained to me. There wouldn't even be a proper wedding for the devoted couple who had known each other forever and had long planned to marry. A small, simple ceremony attended by immediate family was the tasteful, appropriate option they'd chosen. Nevertheless, my mother wanted to let her young friend know that *every* baby's birth was a wonderful event, an occasion to be anticipated and celebrated with joy.

When Mom visited the expectant mother and bride-to-be, armed with baby gifts and a deeply felt compassion that had sprung from her own mother's heart, she taught me a lesson in hospitality I have never forgotten, and a tradition of welcome I try my best to keep.

Most of us practice hospitality because we've learned it from those closest to us. It's part of how we approach the world, like the way we mow the grass or make pasta sauce. Our offerings of hospitality usually reflect family background and early training. But over time, we have the chance to add our own personal touches, to make our own hospitable mark. As we tweak tradition with creative twists on familiar themes, hospitality evolves into a unique expression of our individual personalities and a reflection of our ever-developing interior lives. Identifying traditions of hospitality that have shaped and nurtured us helps us understand the timelessness, the relevance, the attraction of this common sense virtue.

ospitality is part of our tradition. It's found in our families and our churches, in communities that embrace hospitality as a mission and a goal. How we integrate hospitality into our lives is a matter of personal choice. It's up to us to make our own traditions.

conclusion

a reflection

of God's

smiling face

> Our courteous Lord wills
> that we should be
> as at home with him as
> heart may think or soul
> may desire.
>
> JULIAN OF NORWICH

There's a small brown bird who visits me each morning. If I'm sitting on my front porch between seven and eight o'clock, I can usually spy it before my day gets underway. Perched on a metal lamppost in front of a seven-foot camellia bush, the little warbler belts out a concert guaranteed to make the grumpiest riser grin.

I've done nothing to deserve this daily visitation. I've scattered no seed, prepared no bath to lure my feathery friend. I'm just a sleepy-eyed bystander, regularly treated to an uninterrupted solo that takes my breath away. I know some might dismiss the bird's presence with a fleeting nod and casual wave. It's just a bird, after all, and a fairly color-less one at that. Its song, though true and clear, is barely a blip on the audio screen, a tiny voice muffled by mowers, cars, and an occasional barking dog. But for me, the bird is proof that God is interested. God is at work. The bird outside my window is a carrier pigeon with a message from God I'm hard pressed to ignore: *You are loved.*

The God of my understanding is a hospitable God—welcoming, accepting, generous, forgiving. There is compassion in God's face, eagerness in God's open arms, affection in God's smile, and music in God's voice. The bird in my garden is a reminder of God's intimate delight in my existence. I am the apple of God's eye, the darling of God's heart, the favored one. In my humble opinion, *you* are God's favorite, too.

My God is big enough to absorb my inadequacies, to overlook my flaws. God accepts me, even when I find it hard to accept myself. God's hospitality is unswerving, ever-faithful. It's as unconditional as the love of a doting parent, as indulgent as the embrace of a devoted friend, as clear and true as the song of a little brown bird. As I bask in the sunlight of God's overwhelming gifts, enjoying the benefits of God's blessed favor, I'm reminded that I'm called to do as God does, to give as I've been given.

I'm expected to offer unconditional hospitality, even when it doesn't come easily. This implies flexibility and selflessness. It involves openness to inconvenient schedules and offbeat personalities. It means smiling at grouches and those who dress and think differently from me, as well as those I find easy to engage. Accepting, welcoming, and loving others as they are, and not as I want them to be, mirrors God's own unflagging fidelity.

HOSPITALITY PREVAILS

In the aftermath of Hurricane Katrina, the 2005 storm that devastated America's Gulf Coast and wrought unimagined suffering on its people, a group of volunteers from our community aided in the cleanup effort in Long Beach, Mississippi. The losses were overwhelming, the needs far beyond what affected towns and cities could meet on their own. In the face of death and destruction, the presence of hospitality as a response to human tragedy was palpable.

When the group arrived in Long Beach, they were directed to an old roller rink in the process of being converted to a parochial school. The former facility, within walking distance of the ocean, had been leveled like a tower of alphabet blocks. Only a shell remained where once a state of the art educational complex had stood.

"Within days after the hurricane, funds were donated to purchase the skate center. Renovation began immediately," reported my husband, one of six volunteers who'd made the trip. Over the course of three weeks, twelve classrooms were carved out of the wide open skating space. Thanks to the combined efforts of parents, teachers, students, and strangers, the new facility was ready to receive over two hundred children less than a month after the storm surge hit.

The experience of our small band of helpers, so eager to join thousands of like-minded volunteers who surfaced all over Alabama, Mississippi, and Louisiana following the hurricane, dramatically illustrates the power and punch hospitality wields. When they arrived, they were given complimentary housing in a former convent that had been resurrected as a retreat house. There they were offered a send-off breakfast before the eighty-mile drive to their job assignment each day. At the worksite, they were fed lunch and dinner by parents of the schoolchildren—themselves victims of the storm—who expressed their gratitude with hearty casseroles, iced-down beverages, and delicious desserts.

The day school opened, volunteers attended a flag-raising ceremony followed by Mass. "We sat down in the very back row, but were motioned to the front," my husband told me. "It was very biblical." The hardworking volunteers were given a standing ovation and were invited to be gift-bearers for the offertory procession. "After Mass, there were lots of hugs," my husband remembered. "People thanked us and said they were lifted up because of us, but we were lifted up by the hope and hospitality they could still muster in spite of their incredible losses."

Thomas Rodi, the bishop of Biloxi who celebrated Mass that day, had a message of hospitality for the children gathered in their new school for the first time. The building and the sense of normalcy it brought to their lives, he said, were living proof that the students were deeply loved by their parents, their teachers, and the strangers who came to help. "Most of all," Bishop Rodi told the children, "this new school is proof that you are loved by God."

Hospitality is an antidote to despair, a tonic that heals and blesses in the worst of circumstances. What mattered wasn't how much carpet volunteers had laid, not how many desks they'd carried, nor how much cement they had troweled. What mattered was that they showed up toting hospitality in their tool boxes along with their screwdrivers and saws. They were present. They had come to share the burden. As vessels of God's abundant hospitality, they received as much or more than they had given.

BRINGING HOSPITALITY HOME

Sometimes hospitality flows like water from a tap, with a graceful gush and happy gurgle. It comes easily, without struggle or exertion. At other times, hospitality sputters and fizzles like a dampened sparkler on the Fourth of July. It's a tough workout, an exercise I'd prefer to avoid. If I want to sidestep my own capriciousness, I have to treat hospitality like any other virtue. I have to put some thought into it, get my hands dirty. I have to do my part so God can do God's part.

✦   How do I practice hospitality in my everyday life?

✦   What opportunities to practice hospitality have I had over the past year? The past week? Today?

✦   What holds me back from offering hospitality to others? To myself?

✦   Have I asked God to grant me a hospitable heart?

✦   How has the hospitality I've received from others made a difference in my life?

✦   What gifts of hospitality do I possess?

✦   Do I offer as much hospitality to those I live with as I do to others?

✦   Do I bring a spirit of hospitality to my workplace?

✦   Does a tradition of hospitality pervade my home?

✦   Where and with whom do I feel most welcome? Who feels most welcomed by me?

✦   What can I do to integrate hospitality into my spiritual journey?

✦   How can I return God's hospitality by making room for God in my life?

I'm called to reflect the hospitality of a gracious God. I'm asked to go out of my way to accommodate others without neglecting myself. I'm challenged to strike a healthy balance between selfishness and selflessness. I can't do it on my own.

God of windows, God of doors
God of kitchens and dining room chairs,
God of pots and ladles and spoons,
God of nourishment, God of rest,
Help me share the gifts I've been given.

God of the lonely, the hungry, the sad,
God of the children, the aged, the infirm,
God of travelers, strangers, and friends,
God of neighbors, allies, and foes,
Grant me the grace to serve and be served.

God of my family, God of my self,
God of my home, my harvest, my hopes,
Make me a vessel to carry your love,
A quiet echo of your silent embrace.
Create in me a hospitable heart.

Hospitality is a seed planted deep within us that awaits our attention and care. Nurtured by willingness, watered by prayer, hospitality reflects the face of a loving, accepting, compassionate God. Wherever we go, whatever we do, we can pray that a spirit of hospitality will permeate our thoughts and animate our actions.

BIBLIOGRAPHY

Allaire, James, and Rosemary Broughton. *Praying with Dorothy Day*. Winona, MN: St. Mary's Press, 1995.

Benedict of Nursia. *The Rule*. www.osb.org/rb.

Day, Dorothy. *Loaves and Fishes*. San Francisco: Harper and Row, 1963.

———. *The Long Loneliness*. San Francisco: Harper and Row, 1952.

Doherty, Catherine de Hueck. *Poustinia*. Notre Dame, IN: Ave Maria Press, 1983.

Eifler, Jerry. *Linger and Be Available*. Louisville, KY: Butler Book Publishing, 2003.

Gathje, Peter R. *Christ Comes in the Stranger's Guise: A History of the Open Door Community*. Atlanta, GA: Open Door Community, 1991.

Gonzalez-Balado, Jose Luis. *In My Own Words: Mother Teresa's Reflections*. Liguori, MO: Liguori Publications, 1997.

Jarvis, Thea. "A Catholic Worker Day in New York." *The Georgia Bulletin*, October 6, 1983.

———. "Atlanta's Open Door: A Presbyterian Catholic Worker House." *The Georgia Bulletin*, October 6, 1983.

———. "Gamble to Help Troubled Boys Brings Dividends." *The Georgia Bulletin*, June 2, 1988.

Julian of Norwich. *Enfolded in Love: Daily Readings with Julian of Norwich*. New York: Seabury Press, 1981.

Madden, Chris Casson. *A Room of Her Own*. New York: Clarkson Potter, 1997.

———. *Haven*. New York: Clarkson Potter, 2004.

Merton, Thomas. *New Seeds of Contemplation*. New York: New Directions, 1972.

————. *The Waters of Siloe*. Garden City, NY: Garden City Books, 1951.

————. *The Wisdom of the Desert*. New York: New Directions, 1970.

Mother Teresa. Text of remarks delivered June 12, 1995. *The Georgia Bulletin*, June 15, 1995.

Nouwen, Henri. *Bread for the Journey: A Daybook of Wisdom and Faith*. San Francisco: Harper, 1997.

————. *The Path of Peace*. New York: The Crossroad Publishing Company, 1995.

O'Connor, Flannery. *Mystery and Manners*. New York: Farrar, Straus and Giroux, 1969.

Peck, M. Scott. *Meditations from the Road: Daily Reflections from* The Road Less Traveled *and* The Different Drum. New York: Simon and Schuster, 1993.

Pohl, Christine D. *Making Room: Recovering Hospitality as a Christian Tradition*. Grand Rapids, MI: William B. Eerdmans Publishing Company, 1999.

Popson, Martha. *That We Might Have Life*. Garden City, NY: Doubleday and Company, 1981.

Rogers, Fred. *The World According to Mister Rogers*. New York: Hyperion, 2003.

Senior, Jennifer. "The Fireman's Friar." *New York*, November 12, 2001.

Vardeman, John. *On Eagle's Wings: The True Story of the Founding of Eagle Ranch*. Decatur, GA: Looking Glass Books, 1995.

Wiseman, James A., O.S.B. "Three Keys to Lenten Joy." *The Word Among Us*, Lent, 2005.

photo by David Miller

THEA JARVIS has written for numerous periodicals, including *The Atlanta Constitution*, *America Magazine*, *Catholic Digest*, and *Catholic News Service*. For nineteen years she wrote for the *Georgia Bulletin*, Atlanta's Catholic weekly newspaper. Her family life column was featured in seventeen diocesan newspapers. She is also the author of *The Gift of Grandparenting* (Sorin Books).

Sabbath Presence

Appreciating the Gifts of Each Day
Kathleen Casey

These thirteen reflections, each with Scripture, a meditation activity, and meditation questions, invite us to explore the gifts of Sabbath, a time apart from our busy everyday lives when we can get to know God, explore values, contemplate life's big questions, and express love and gratitude.

ISBN: 1-59471-068-6 / 128 pages / $10.95
Ave Maria Press

Revised Edition!
Touching the Holy

Ordinariness, Self-Esteem and Friendship
Robert J. Wicks

Robert J. Wicks offers fresh insights into the spirituality and psychology of sound self-esteem and real friendship. He suggests that the simplicity and openness of truly ordinary people is a meeting place with God. Truly ordinary people, he believes, are those "who have the courage and trust in God to simply be themselves."

ISBN: 1-933495-02-2 / 192 pages / $12.95
Ave Maria Press

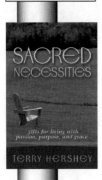

Sacred Necessities

Gifts for Living with Passion, Purpose, and Grace
Terry Hershey

What is it that makes life worth living? What makes the everyday, ordinary world extraordinary—even sacred? If we want to be truly alive there are a few things we really need, a few sacred necessities: Amazement, Sanctuary, Stillness, Grace, Simplicity, Resilience, and Friendship. This is not simply a prescription for the good life; rather, it is a gentle nudge to live with an open heart and a willing spirit.

ISBN: 1-893732-93-2 / 192 pages / $14.95
Sorin Books

ave maria press

Available from your bookstore or from
ave maria press / Notre Dame, IN 46556
www.avemariapress.com / Ph: 800-282-1865
A Ministry of the Indiana Province of Holy Cross

Prices and availability subject to change   Keycode: FØTØ1Ø7ØØØØ